D0955262

PENGUIN BOOKS

JANE AUSTEN

Carol Shields (1935–2003) is the author of *Dressing Up for the Carnival; Larry's Party*, which won the Orange Prize; and *The Stone Diaries*, which won the 1995 Pulitzer Prize for Fiction and the National Book Critics Circle Award. Her other novels and short-story collections include *The Republic of Love, Happenstance, Swann, The Orange Fish, Various Miracles, The Box Garden*, and *Small Ceremonies* (all available from Penguin).

Praise for *Jane Austen*

"Short but delightful biography . . . Austen died at forty-one . . . kept no diary, never sat for a professional portrait, did not marry, did not travel, and lived an austerely private existence. In short, she is a mystery, one that Shields explores with the patience and empathy of a devoted fan." —*The Atlanta Journal-Constitution*

"Carol Shields has distilled the essential Jane Austen into a slender volume that focuses on the writer's life, that interior space that Shields knows intimately and analyzes brilliantly. . . . Shields provides an insider's view of the writer's world—which is what makes this biography so compelling."
—*The Philadelphia Inquirer*

"Shields reconstructs [Austen's] life in insightful, detailed prose."
—*The New York Times Book Review*

"[A] shrewd pairing of subject and author." —*Chicago Sun-Times*

"Carol Shields, whose novels are often about quiet lives, has done something impressive with her compact *Jane Austen*. She's created a fully dimensioned portrait of Austen from a record that is sporadic and fragmented." —*The Charlotte Observer*

"Penguin's wonderful series of 'lives' . . . delights once again, this time with a pithy literary biography of Jane Austen by Pulitzer Prize–winning fiction writer Shields . . . With frankness, warmth

and grace, Shields writes of an 'opaque' subject who lived a short life and about whom very little is known beyond family letters."
—*Publishers Weekly*

"[Austen] once said, 'If a book is well written, I always find it too short.' So it is with Shields's delicate analysis of Austen's life and artistry: As with any life of Jane Austen, we can only complain that it ends too soon."
—*The Boston Globe*

"It's a quiet, self-effacing little book, but underneath lies the delight of one fierce intelligence considering another."
—*The Vancouver Sun* (British Columbia)

"Austen herself was such a prodigious chronicler of the social scenes in which she lived that one might wonder if there is any more to say about them. For the legions of Austen lovers, it is nice to know that answer is a resounding 'yes.'"
—*Tampa Tribune*

"[Shields] has written a classic study of how great fiction is created."
—*The London Free Press*

"[Shields] brings a particularly perceptive and sympathetic eye to the details of Austen's life, and a fresh way of telling the tale."
—*The Buffalo News*

"[Shields's] book is an engaging, beautifully written and opinionated view of a writer many people just can't get enough of."
—*The Gazette* (Montreal)

"[Shields's] biography is lively and engaging and should be a welcome addition to scholarship on Austen."
—*The Vindicator* (Youngstown, Ohio)

"Any fan of Jane Austen, from fifteen to ninety-five, can expect to enjoy this book—no Ph.D. required."
—*Calgary Herald*

"Shields's study is a little treasure."
—*Daily Mail*

CAROL SHIELDS

Jane Austen

A Penguin Life

A LIPPER™/ PENGUIN BOOK

PENGUIN BOOKS

Published by the Penguin Group

Penguin Group (USA) Inc., 375 Hudson Street, New York, New York 10014, U.S.A.
Penguin Group (Canada), 10 Alcorn Avenue, Toronto, Ontario, Canada M4V 3B2
(a division of Pearson Penguin Canada Inc.)
Penguin Books Ltd, 80 Strand, London WC2R 0RL, England
Penguin Ireland, 25 St Stephen's Green, Dublin 2, Ireland
(a division of Penguin Books Ltd)
Penguin Group (Australia), 250 Camberwell Road, Camberwell, Victoria 3124,
Australia (a division of Pearson Australia Group Pty Ltd)
Penguin Books India Pvt Ltd, 11 Community Centre, Panchsheel Park,
New Delhi - 110 017, India
Penguin Group (NZ), cnr Airborne and Rosedale Roads, Albany, Auckland 1310,
New Zealand (a division of Pearson New Zealand Ltd)
Penguin Books (South Africa) (Pty) Ltd, 24 Sturdee Avenue, Rosebank,
Johannesburg 2196, South Africa

Penguin Books Ltd, Registered Offices:
80 Strand, London WC2R 0RL, England

First published in the United States of America by Penguin Group (USA),
a member of Penguin Putnam, Inc. 2001
Published in Penguin Books 2005

5 7 9 10 8 6 4

THE LIBRARY OF CONGRESS HAS CATALOGED THE
HARDCOVER EDITION AS FOLLOWS:
Shields, Carol.
Jane Austen / Carol Shields.
p. cm.–(A Penguin life)
ISBN 0-670-89488-5 (hc.)
ISBN 0 14 30.3516 9 (pbk.)
1. Austen, Jane, 1775–1817.   2. Novelists, English–19th century–Biography.   I. Title.
II. Penguin lives series.
PR4036.S48   2001
823'.7–dc21
[B]   00-043807

Printed in the United States of America
Set in Caslon Book
Designed by Francesca Belanger

For Hazel and for Grace

Prologue: A Life Glimpsed

IN THE AUTUMN of 1996 my daughter, the writer Anne Giardini, and I traveled to Richmond, Virginia, to present a joint paper at the Jane Austen Society of North America, an organization that comprises some of the world's most respected Austen scholars, as well as rank amateurs like ourselves. These affectionate annual gatherings are serious attempts to look at Jane Austen's work and examine how it illuminates her time and ours. There is minimal incense burning at these meetings, and no attempt to trivialize Jane Austen's pronouncements and mockingly bring her into our contemporary midst. The gatherings are both gentle in approach and rigorous in scholarship, and unlike many academic assemblies, they are festivals of inclusiveness, with middle-aged groupies from Detroit dressed in Regency costumes; keen-eyed, tenured professors from Canada; and a scattering of Europeans intent on winning the trivia quiz. (Wherever three or four come together in Jane Austen's name, there is bound to be a trivia quiz. This detailing of Austen's minor characters—what they ate for breakfast, how much income they've settled on their daughters, the precise hour of a ruined picnic—has never been a part of my own impressionistic response to her work, and I worry, but only a little, about what this says of me, her devoted reader.)

The subject for the 1996 conference was "Jane Austen's Men," but the presentation Anne and I had prepared kept slipping sideways into the fully gendered world and coasting toward the subject of how women, despite their societal disentitlement, were able to play such a lively, even powerful role. The Austen heroines, deprived of the right to speak, employ the intricacies of body language–a term not invented until the 1960s, but no matter. Jane Austen was familiar with the body's vivid mechanics and relied heavily, especially in her dramatic conclusions, on the body's expressiveness.

Our talk centered on what Anne and I called the "politics of the glance." If, in an Austen novel, a woman's tongue is obliged to be still, her eye becomes her effective agent, one piercing look capable of changing the narrative direction– even a half glance able to shame or empower or redirect the sensibilities of others.

A glance can both submit and subvert; it can be sharp or shy, scornful or adoring; it can be a near cousin to scrutiny– but it almost always assumes a degree of mutually encoded knowledge. A spark is struck and apprehended; the head turns on its spinal axis; the shoulders freeze; the eyes are the only busy part of the body, simultaneously receiving and sending out information, so that a glance becomes more than a glance. It is a weapon, a command, or a sigh of acquiescence.

After the conference Anne and I traveled separately to

our homes, I to central Canada and she to Vancouver. In Chicago, Anne was obliged to change planes, and she was amused to find that her new seatmate had come fresh from the annual Napoléon conference in that city. Riding high over the clouds, they exchanged conference notes, and the Napoléon man challenged her, not at all to her surprise, on the fact that Jane Austen had commented so scantily on the unfolding history of her era.

We've heard this often: How could a novelist who writes astutely about her own immediate society fail to have mentioned the Napoleonic wars?

The modeling of war is mostly male—almost everyone would agree on this and on the truth that war's exactitude and damage may elude a conventional fictional transaction. But shouldn't Jane Austen at least have mentioned one battle or general by name? Why is there not a word about the rapidly evolving mercantile class and the new democratization of Britain? What about changes in political structure, in the power and persuasion of the Church, in the areas of science and medicine? These questions are often challengingly presented, as though novels are compilations of "current events" and Jane Austen a frivolous, countrified person in intellectual drag, impervious to the noises of the historical universe in which she was placed.

In fact, Jane Austen covers all these matters, if not with the directness and particularity our Napoléon man might have liked. Her novels, each of them, can be seen as wide-ranging *glances*—that "g" word again, with its tune of deliberation–across the material of the world she inhabited, and that material includes an implied commentary on the political, economic, and social forces of her day. These glances, like ubiquitous sunlight, sweep and suggest, excoriate and question. The soldiers who distract the Bennet sisters in *Pride and Prejudice* are posted nearby in case of an invasion from France–why else would they be there?–and their presence threatens the stability of local society, a sociological certainty that was fully comprehended by the author of six novels written over a stretch of unsettled time, each of them offering its historical commentary.

By indirection, by assumption, by reading what is implicit, we can find behind Austen's novels a steady, intelligent witness to a world that was rapidly reinventing itself. Every Austen conversation, every chance encounter on a muddy road, every evening of cards before the fire, every bold, disruptive militiaman is backed by historical implication. For even the most casual reader, the period of Austen's life, 1775–1817, becomes visible through her trenchant, knowing glance. That glance may be hard-edged or soft, part of a novel's texture or backdrop, or it may constitute the raw energy of propulsion. It is never accidental. For the biographer, one such "glance" is multiplied a thousand times. Austen's short life may have been lived in relative privacy, but her novels show her to be a citizen, and certainly a spectator, of a far wider world.

1

TODAY JANE AUSTEN belongs to the nearly unreachable past. She kept no diary that we know of. There is no voice recording such as we possess of Virginia Woolf, and no photograph like the one that George Eliot denied she had had taken—but which remains in the records, proclaiming her an indisputably unhandsome woman.

Austen's intractable silences throw long shadows on her apparent chattiness. In part, the opacity of her life may rest on the degree to which it was fused with that of her sister Cassandra, providing a mask or at the very least a subsuming presence. Each sister's life invaded the other, canceling out parts of the knowable self. (Cassandra once famously described her sister as "the sun of my life, the gilder of every pleasure, the soother of every sorrow.") The accidental adjacency of these two sisters reaches out and shapes each of their lives, and at the same time informs the novels of the younger sister and asks persistent questions about the nature of the creative act. How does art emerge? How does art come from common clay, in this case a vicar's self-educated daughter, all but buried in rural Hampshire? Who was she really? And who exactly is her work designed to please? One person? Two or three? Or an immense, wide, and unknown audience that buzzes with an altered frequency through changing generations, its impact subtly augmented in the light of newly evolved tastes and values?

One hundred sixty Austen letters survive, but none written earlier than her twentieth year. Many other letters were destroyed by Cassandra after Jane Austen died, and we can surmise with some certainty that the jettisoned letters were the most revealing and riveting. Somehow we never hear quite enough of Jane Austen's off-guard voice. Her insistent irony blunts rather than sharpens her tone. Descriptions of herself are protective when they are not disarming, and her sketches of others are frequently arch or else cruel. She writes quickly so that the text will mimic the sound of her own voice, a letter-writing technique that was encouraged in her time, and so the scattered and somewhat breathless nature of her correspondence is not the result of carelessness but of deliberation.

Of the eight Austen children, there were only two who were not honored by portraits: Jane and her handicapped brother, George. Cassandra produced the two informal sketches we have of Jane Austen. One is a rather unattractive back view–round-shouldered, dumpy–and the other shows a woman whose curved cheeks and small straight mouth give a slightly absent, querulous air of sad reasonableness. She is looking sideways in this portrait, perhaps at that lack of event that was said to characterize her life. Her niece Anna, who adored her, wrote admiringly about Aunt Jane's various features, saying: "One hardly understands how with all these advantages she could yet fail of being a decidedly handsome woman." Meaning, clearly, that she was not a beauty, though mercifully she had escaped the smallpox that disfigured so many of her contemporaries. A family friend spoke of the childlike expression in her face, so "lively and full of humour." Various accounts refer to the slightness of her figure, and several mention the liveliness of her movements, her quickness of step. Was she dark or fair? There is wide variation even on this topic by near and distant witnesses, but a lock owned by a descendant of Jane Austen confirms that she had curly dark-brown hair mixed with a few strands of gray. A neighbor, the renowned writer Mary Russell Mitford, rather maliciously compared her to a poker, "perpendicular, precise, taciturn."

Jane Austen's appearance is of interest to the reader partly because it satisfies a curiosity we all feel, but chiefly because it is known that, at the time, exceptional beauty occasionally gave an advantage to women of little means, which is exactly what Jane Austen was. Beauty had value, as it always has: Seductive powers were informally factored into the dowry arrangement. Intelligence, on the other hand, was more likely to present a negative weight. Intelligent women could not always be kept under control, and control was a husband's obligation.

A writer of "marriage novels," Austen did not marry, and it must be wondered to what extent her looks, handsome or unhandsome, played a part in that destiny. A silhouette has been found in recent years that seemed to connect, along an ambiguous pathway, with a fine-featured and "pretty" Jane Austen. The hopeful excitement this image stirred was extraordinary, indicating the affection in which Austen is held; readers, and perhaps scholars too, appeared eager to believe that she was, after all, favorably disposed, since that would mean she had more power over her choices, and that Cassandra, as portraitist, was unreliable or even vindictive as a sisterly witness, as many have suspected. Unfortunately, the identity of the silhouette has remained unproven.

Jane Austen is recognized for her moral sensibility, and for what is assumed to be her rare ability to expand insignificant material, turning the doings of a few village families into wide-screen drama. Critical commentary has often served her poorly, rarely posing the question of whether she knew what she was doing. Her solid writerly advice to her scribbling nieces and nephew should convince us absolutely that she did. "You are now collecting your People delightfully," she wrote her niece Anna, "getting them exactly into such a spot as is the delight of my life;–3 or 4 Families in a Country Village is the very thing to work on." She also warned Anna about such novelistic clichés as "vortex of Dissipation." To her nephew James Edward Austen-Leigh, another hopeful writer, she referred to her own writing as "the little bit (two inches wide) of ivory on which I work with so fine a Brush, as produces little effect after much labour."

She is being self-deprecating here; her trust in the microcosmic world is securely placed. It is also a brave and original view. Out of her young, questioning self came the grave certainty that the family was the source of art, just as every novel is in a sense about the fate of a child. It might be argued that all literature is ultimately about family, the creation of structures—drama, poetry, fiction—that reflect our immediate and randomly assigned circle of others, what families do to us and how they can be reimagined or transcended.

She is also—and the vagueness of this perception is baffling—widely believed to be someone possessed of a small soul marked by a profound psychic wound. This is an idea that has become enameled and precious and ready for museum sanctity. The defensive tone of her letters and the cheerful mockery that characterizes her unsentimental novels support this belief to a point, but we can only guess at the degree of her alienation or its cause. It might amount to little more than simple contagion. She lived, after all, in an age of satire, and as near as we know, she was the child of unsentimental parents.

Scholars can't even agree on what to call her. This is a messy problem and not a new one in the field of biography. The biographer and scholar John Halperin calls her, mostly, "the novelist," which is terrifyingly respectful but also reductive, and just slightly obsequious. "Jane" itself feels too familiar an address to apply to the adult writer, although it is found everywhere in the more recent biographies. Jane is also what Jane Austen's nephew James Edward Austen-Leigh resorts to on occasion in his famous memoir written long after his aunt's death, and the reader can feel the struggle this very conservative nineteenth-century male is suffering while trying to find a proper form of address for his aunt Jane. Ms. Austen is unthinkable. Miss Austen? No! (Cassandra as the older sister claims that title.) Austen on its own possesses an indelicacy; we know, somehow, that she would have been offended. Like a literary butler, the biographer is obliged to weigh the options and employ the unsatisfactory Jane or else repeat the whole name again and again–Jane Austen–or rely on the clumsiness of treasonous pronouns.

Another problem a biographer of Jane Austen faces is how to proceed without sounding like Jane Austen. The cadence is catching, and so is the distancing "one" voice, as in "one thinks," "one observes." Her equivocations, so sprawling, thoughtful, and "correct," conflict with what we like to think of as a stern critical eye. Her reflectiveness, that calm, deliberate voice, hums in the background, deflecting analysis and telling us to disappear, please, so that the novel can get underway. Biography zaps the enchantment of the writing itself by throwing a profile of theory against a text–that crisp and useful word–that had no immediate acquaintance with literary theory. This is, in the end, what matters: the novels themselves, and not the day-to-day life of the author, the cups of tea she sipped with her neighbors, the cream cakes she bought at a bakery. Even her extraordinarily revealing letters must be separated–somehow–from the works of fiction that have survived. The novelist George Gissing wrote that "the only good biographies are to be found in novels." He was speaking about the genuine arc of a human life, that it can perhaps be presented more authentically in fiction than in the genre of biography. Biography is subject to warps and gaps and gasps of admiration or condemnation, but fiction respects the human trajectory.

Traditionally Jane Austen's biographers have nailed together the established facts of her life—her birth, her travels, her enthusiasms, her death—and clothed this rickety skeleton with speculation gleaned from the novels, an exercise akin to ransacking an author's bureau drawers and drawing conclusions from piles of neatly folded handkerchiefs or worn gloves. In so doing, the assumption is made that fiction flows directly from a novelist's experience rather than from her imagination. The series of troubled families in the Austen novels, for instance, has been seen as a reflection of Jane Austen's own presumably disordered domestic space. It is easy enough, after reading the novels, to imagine fierce sibling rivalry in the Austen clan or even the petty irritations that accumulate when numbers of adults and children are confined during the course of a few rainy days. But to employ the word "dysfunctional" when describing the Austens points to a parallel difficulty in which contemporary ideas and terms are perceived as being timeless. They are not. The late-eighteenth-century mind did not work along the same track as ours today, and I have attempted in this short life of Jane Austen to read *into* my own resistance, instead of seeking a confirmation or denial embedded in the fiction.

Jane Austen was born in the remote Hampshire village of Steventon, with its fewer than thirty families, on the sixteenth of December 1775. Her parents, George Austen, Rector of Steventon, and his wife, Cassandra Leigh Austen, belonged to what was then called the lesser gentry. The couple was not, in their early years, or perhaps ever, economically secure, but their level of education and family connections meant that they were not at a disadvantage when set beside their wealthier neighbors.

The continuance of the Austen family line was a concern, but it is unlikely that the Austens, George and Cassandra, were disappointed that their seventh child should be a girl. The rectory was full of little boys, all born in quick succession, and Jane was welcomed as a playmate for the Austens' only other daughter, two-year-old Cassandra.

No doctor was required for the birth—in fact, there was no doctor in the village—but Mrs. Austen was undoubtedly attended by her sister-in-law Philadelphia, who was visiting at the time, along with Aunt Philadelphia's fourteen-year-old daughter, Eliza. The winter that followed was exceptionally long and bitter according to surviving records, and probably it was this hardship that postponed young Jane's formal christening until the spring of 1776.

Her first months were spent indoors, snug at the breast of her mother. Mrs. Austen's parenting ideas were unorthodox, for unlike many contemporaries of her class, she believed in breast-feeding her babies for a few months in order to give them a good start. After weaning, though, the children were placed in the hands of a local family, probably the Littleworth family at nearby Cheesedown Farm, until they reached what Mrs. Austen considered to be the age of reason, that is until they could walk and talk and demonstrate a measure of sturdy independence.

The length of time during which Jane would have been fostered out is not known, but it can be imagined that the abrupt shift from mother's breast to alien household made a profound emotional impact on the child. This early expulsion from home was the first of many, and it is doubtful whether she had much to say about such later separations, just as she had little power over her other domestic arrangements. Sharing a bedroom all her life, she was denied the "heaven" that Emily Dickinson found in her solitary upstairs space. Her fictional expression can be imagined as a smooth flow of narrative deriving from her confined reality, but a flow that is interrupted by jets of alternate possibility, the moment observed and then repositioned and recharged.

More and more, to the contemporary sensibility, it seems that the true subject of serious fiction is not "current events," ongoing wars or political issues, but the search of an individual for his or her true home. Men and women, in fiction and in life, become separated from their home; in the novels of Jane Austen they are misdirected or misassigned, so that home, both in its true and metaphorical sense, becomes a desired but denied destination. At the same time Jane Austen herself must often have felt almost more homeless when she was restricted to home than when she was banished from it.

The sensitive (some would say pious) Fanny Price in *Mansfield Park* is born, it would appear, into a family of aliens—a drinking father, an indifferent mother—and must do with this situation what she can. Elizabeth Bennet of *Pride and Prejudice* is, though she doesn't put it quite so plainly, ashamed of her parents, possessing a sensibility that seeks its fulfillment in the creation of a new home with Darcy. Emma Woodhouse can be thought of as a half orphan, unable to grow up until she finds a path to making a home of her own. And Jane Austen herself, laboring over her brilliant fictions, creates again and again a vision of refuge furnished with love, acceptance, and security, an image she herself would be able to call a home of her own.

2

JANE AUSTEN CHOSE to focus her writing on daughters rather than mothers (with the exception of her short and curious novel *Lady Susan*), but nevertheless mothers are essential in her fiction. They are the engines that push the action forward, even when they fail to establish much in the way of maternal warmth. Daughters achieve their independence by working against the family constraints, their young spirits struck from the passive, lumpish postures of their ineffectual or distanced mothers. Elizabeth Bennet (*Pride and Prejudice*), the most transparent example, is everything that her foolish mother is not. The feeble Mrs. Dashwood in *Sense and Sensibility* leans on her three daughters rather than supporting them; the good woman is respected, but we know, and Jane Austen knows, that she is powerless. Emma's mother is an absence, a vague memory, as one would expect the enfeebled spouse of Mr. Woodhouse to be, and Emma's mothering has been handed over to a hired surrogate, Mrs. Weston, who not surprisingly wants to have a life and a child of her own— even though this leaves the hapless, ill-equipped Emma attempting to mother the whole village of Highbury with her plots and dramas. *Northanger Abbey,* which can be read as a coming-of-age novel, shows Mrs. Morland to be a good but rather casual mother, neglecting the matter of her daughter Catherine's moral development and such important issues as how to distinguish the real world from its romantic shadow. And Lady Russell, Anne Elliot's well-meaning, prudent surrogate mother in *Persuasion*, actively interferes, urging Anne to reject her suitor, Captain Wentworth, and thereby launching the novel's action.

A close bond between mothers and daughters is rare in the Austen novels, but then mothering styles are forever in a state of change. The sentimental, smothering mother of Victorian fiction had not yet evolved. Childhood, too, has its different modes and expectations, and it was almost certainly shorter in the eighteenth century than it is today, with a brief period of innocent dependency followed by rapid absorption into adult society.

Of Jane Austen's mother we know only a little. She was an accomplished versifier all her life, delighting in rhymes and rhythm, and her light verse, even after all these years and even considering the private references, still gives pleasure. Suggested glimpses of hypochondria or peevishness envelop her in later life—each of these glimpses gestures toward and secures a hundred others, as is often the case when biographical documentation is scarce. Jane Austen, in her final illness, reports she was too weak to walk upstairs and so she sometimes rested on three sitting-room chairs lined up together, leaving the sofa for her mother. What can we make of this improbable scene? Did her mother not notice the unusual furniture deployment? Or was Jane Austen in the full throes of a bizarre martyrdom? Were the mother and daughter playing out an old and rivalrous claim? Or was Mrs. Austen—and this is the interpretation that has hardened in the record—a demanding and self-absorbed woman, careless of her daughter's comfort and too insensitive to see the signs of serious illness?

Jane Austen wrote to her sister Cassandra, in what looks like a dropped comment but which, examined, holds an armful of meaning: "I like the Gown very much & my Mother thinks it very ugly." The balance of that particular sentence suggests an imbalance of sensibility. The repetition of the word "very" forms a kind of code that Cassandra would be sure to understand. Mrs. Austen was geared to opposition, to stances that were negative.

We do know she was a strong, clever woman from a slightly higher ledge of the gentry than her husband, that she was occasionally caustic in the verses she wrote, and later, like Mrs. Bennet, was anxious about her unmarried daughters. But how could she not have been, and have we as readers been completely fair to Mrs. Bennet of *Pride and Prejudice*? A good marriage was the only real hope for young women of Mrs. Bennet's class, though marriage, with its new dangers and surrenders, often presented a form of martyrdom. Mrs. Bennet, always broadly played on the screen, may, in fact, be something of a solid realist, embedded in her economic matrix, concerned, and with Darwinian reason, about her nest of unmarried daughters. Her husband, on the other hand, affectionately put forward in film, is seen on close textual inspection to be foolish in his own particularly fastidious and reluctant manner. His wife urges him to call on the newly arrived, large-fortuned Mr. Bingley, but he turns this advice away with sarcastic humor and reserve, and yet we suspect—we know!—he is going to make that call. He is, after all, the straitened father of five daughters; he understands as well as Mrs. Bennet that the call is necessary.

Mrs. Bennet is also the only family member to welcome Lydia back home after her scandalous elopement. This cry of triumph has been interpreted as social pride on her part: At last she has one married daughter, at last she can hold up her head. But there is something of loyalty here as well: a mother's rejoicing in a daughter's happiness, a mother's forgiveness of outrageous and shameful behavior, a generosity that prevails against the rest of the family's hardness of heart. Even Elizabeth is immune to Lydia's happiness, closer to being contemptuous and ashamed.

Mrs. Austen, Jane Austen's mother, may or may not have had a spirit similar to Mrs. Bennet's. However little we know about her, we can be certain she was a preoccupied woman, since an eighth child, Charles, followed not long after Jane's birth, enlarging an already bursting household. The vegetable garden, the dairy—the family kept five cows—and the poultry yard would also have been among Mrs. Austen's responsibilities, as was the supervision of enormous family meals.

The parsonage at Steventon, where Jane Austen was to live for the first twenty-five years of her life, was a large, respectable, but rather plain dwelling. The reception rooms on the ground floor showed their honest whitewashed beams, as well as a host of other architectural inelegancies, though the setting of the house, with its sundial, its flowers and hedgerows and rustic seats, was said to have been exceptionally charming.

Certainly the interior space was commodious enough to contain the boys' boarding school run by the Austens. The Reverend George Austen, Jane's father, was headmaster and sole teacher in the school, and Mrs. Austen supported the endeavor with her good will and practical assistance, overseeing the boys' laundry and offering cheerful encouragement.

Mr. Austen was considered to be a handsome man and one who lived close to the ideal of a country gentleman, occupied with farm and parish duties, at the same time pursuing his scholarly and scientific interests. By all accounts he was a family man, a good father with a genuine interest in his offspring—he himself had been orphaned by the age of nine—and an admirable tolerance for his children's differences, directing them down varying paths: the Church, the Admiralty, or in daughter Jane's case, a life of literature. A farewell letter to his son Francis, off to the East Indies, survives, full of moral and practical advice, mild in tone, yet loving in its construction. Prudence, he told Francis, "will teach you the proper disposal of your time and the careful management of your money—two very important trusts." (This letter from father to son was found with Francis's papers when he died in his nineties, much creased and worn from rereading, a testimony of respect and love.)

The number of students at Steventon was small enough to make the school a family enterprise. Mr. Austen supervised the boys' Greek and Latin in the parlor, to the accompaniment of everyday domestic buzz, visitors coming and going, and the younger children tumbling about. A household of this size, the ten Austens along with their four or five student boarders, ensured a lively ambience and what was most certainly an atmosphere of boisterousness and perhaps, for the young Jane, even ravishing happiness. Boys' games, boys' jokes, boys' inevitable horseplay—all this made the Austens different from the more restrained families of their acquaintance, and young Jane and Cassandra were undoubtedly offered liberties that other girls were denied. They would have shared, too, in the overspill of earnest scholarship—privy to their father's library, invited to observe his globe of the world and peer at natural mysteries through his microscope.

Jane Austen, describing the childhood of Catherine Morland in *Northanger Abbey*, might be touching on her own early years of lightly supervised freedom, years of being "noisy and wild," of playing with balls instead of dolls, of rainy days spent in the barn and family theatricals shared with the wider neighborhood. Such a childhood may well have given her understanding and sympathy for the way in which young male energy is transformed into gentleness and gallantry, a characteristic of all her male heroes.

A childhood is shaped by the presence or nonpresence of siblings. Jane Austen's sister and six brothers, all of whom lived to adulthood, made her the person she was, a privileged observer of close family connections and inevitable conflicts. In addition to the immediate family there were engaging, affectionate neighbors who took an interest in the young Austens. Letters arrived from Aunt Philadelphia, bringing a whiff of a more cosmopolitan world. The seasons came and went; Christmas 1782, when Jane was seven, was celebrated with a play, *Matilda*, put on by the older Austen boys, the first of many family theatricals.

On the whole it can be said that warmth and respect marked the Austen household, but at the same time the family structure was slowly changing. The first son, James, ten years older than Jane, enrolled at Oxford in 1779, leaving some breathing space for the newly born Charles. Another brother, Edward, formed an attachment with the wealthy, distantly related Thomas Knight family of Godmersham, an arrangement that would eventually lead to his formal adoption. A farm refuge was found for another brother, George, who suffered from an unknown disability, probably a form of brain damage or deafness or both.

The idyllic life at Steventon ended abruptly when it was decided that Jane, aged seven, should be sent away to boarding school along with Cassandra and their cousin, Jane Cooper. Whether this decision was made with reflection or through lack of thought is not known, but the transition from country to city life can only have been shocking to so young a child; from rural Hampshire she went to Oxford, and later Southampton, as a pupil in a school run by Mrs. Cawley, whom the family knew only casually. The loss of freedom and the sense of banishment were imprinted on young Jane, and she spoke scathingly of girls' schools and schoolmistresses for the rest of her life. Rescue came in the form of an illness, referred to as a "putrid fever," which sent both sisters home to their indulgent parents.

After a brief interlude the two sisters were sent away once again, this time to the Abbey School in Reading, romantically situated in a ruined twelfth-century monastery where the headmistress, Mrs. La Tournelle, spoke not a word of French, despite her name. Other mistresses did teach a little French as well as some drawing and needlework, and almost certainly dancing. The doors of universities were closed to females, and girls' education in Jane Austen's time consisted of what might be called "accomplishments." The atmosphere of the Abbey School was relaxed, even indolent, and might well have resembled Mrs. Goddard's School in *Emma,* a harmless social construct in which young girls were exposed to healthful food, outdoor exercise, and a less than rigorous academic program. Such establishments served a need in their time. Progressive families were often unguided about what to do with their bright young daughters, who required the connection with learning but not the expectations that might follow. Mr. Austen, perhaps, thought the curriculum at the Abbey School too light for the amount of tuition he was paying; he brought both girls home near the end of 1786, shortly before Jane's eleventh birthday, marking the end of her formal education.

At home conditions were more invigorating than at any girls' school. There were interesting new neighbors, particularly Anne Lefroy, a spirited, learned woman, enormously admired by young Jane Austen. Jane's oldest brother, James, still at Oxford, was often at home, producing ambitious theatricals in the barn, and it is quite possible that Jane took a role in an enactment of Sheridan's *The Rivals*. More interesting yet was the arrival at Christmas, 1786, of Jane's French-speaking cousin Eliza, who had been born in India to Philadelphia Austen Hancock, and was now married herself to a French count, Jean de Feuillide, and the mother of an infant son, Hastings. The household at Steventon was transformed during the visit of these exotic relations by a dose of French worldliness that affected all the Austens and enchanted, especially, young Jane. French manners, French books, French attitudes widened the intellectual and social reach of the family, enlivening routine life.

There were more family theatricals in the following years, in which Jane almost certainly took part. And, at the same time, she was reading. Everything we know about the family tells us that her reading was likely to have been unsupervised and random. Her father's bookshelves would have been open to her, and probably this good-hearted, busy man did not trouble to direct her choices. There existed very little that might be called children's writing, and so she plunged directly into the adult world of letters. Not much is known about what she read, except for Dr. Johnson's essays from *The Rambler* and La Fontaine's *Fables choisies* in French, brought to her as a gift by her cousin Eliza.

More important, when considering the life of Jane

Austen, is that all the family read novels, a form that must have seemed to them very much as early television struck its mid-twentieth-century audience. The Austens, as far as we can tell, were not particularly discriminating, enjoying inferior novels alongside the works of Richardson and Fielding. Established novelists, junk novelists, writers of romance— these classifications had not in the late eighteenth century been firmly established. Even as a child Jane Austen seemed to be thinking of herself as a future novelist, and one who would create more resilient characters than those drawn by the popular writer Mary Brunton, the author of *Self-Control*. Austen wrote, comparing herself to Brunton: "My Heroine shall not merely be wafted down an American river in a boat by herself, she shall cross the Atlantic in the same way, and never stop till she reaches Gravesend."

The novel as a form was in its infancy, and the wonder of the new genre blunted criticism, for here on the page were living, reflective men and women facing real predicaments and expressing genuine desire. Here, in fact, was all that was immediately knowable: families, love affairs, birth and death, boredom and passion, the texture of the quotidian set side by side with the extremities of the human spirit. And here, too, was the specter of a woman's future, the great questions over which there was little control: Was it better to be alone and in some sense intact? Or better to be coupled—and compromised, denied freedom but awarded the respect of society?

3

JANE AUSTEN'S NOVELS are about intelligent women who take themselves seriously, but not solemnly. Each of the Austen heroines possesses an implicit moral system and an impulse toward improvement that seems to require no exposition or justification, no wrestling with ethical dilemmas, no laborious arrivals at the gates of perception. A steadiness of nerve prevails. The perfection of behavior, the refinement of sensibility—these were the natural conditions Jane Austen urged upon her men and women and upon us, her readers.

The young often read Austen's novels as love stories. Later, more knowing readers respond to their intricate structures, their narrative drive, their quiet insistence that we keep turning over the page even though we know the ending, which is invariably one of reconciliation and a projection of future happiness in the form of marriage. But what did marriage mean in the context of these novels? Not a mere exchange of vows repeated in church. Marriage reached beyond its moment of rhetoric and gestured, eloquently and also innocently, toward the only pledge a young woman was capable of giving. She had one chance in her life to say "I do," and these words rhyme psychologically with the phrase: I am, I exist.

Still later, readers come to appreciate the novels' comic brilliance, laughing out loud not just at situations, but at turns of phrase. As a whole, Jane Austen's work presents a consummate artistry that is almost impossible to deconstruct, but which revolves around the fusing of moral seriousness with comic drama. Jane Austen's writing with its wit, elegance, and narrative control outshone that of her contemporaries and those Victorian novelists who came after her. It is almost as though she reinvented and stabilized the wobbly eighteenth-century novel–which seemed unable to stare at itself, to *know* itself–and made it into a modern form.

The novel, though a relatively late literary innovation, almost immediately crowded other forms aside. Its roots can be traced to travel writing, to essays, to narrative poetry, to lives of the saints, and to the French or Italian novella, but as a form it went off like a firecracker in the 1740s with the work of Richardson and Fielding. Here, unapologetically, was the texture of real life on the page; here were men and women whose dilemmas resembled our own. The novel's invention also coincided, happily, with a new widespread literacy among women, making it the only form in which women participated fully, from the beginning. True, the novel's instant popularity gave it something of an inferiority complex; the fact that it explored moral issues indirectly, and with shades of human ambiguity, separated it from more formalized, traditional prose. Serialization distorted some early novelistic experiments, and there was a natural—even moral—confusion over the nature of fiction, its viability, its relationship with the authentic world, how it might be framed, and how seriously it might take itself.

Luckily, the Austen family of Steventon embraced the novel form and welcomed it rather uncritically, it seems, especially the sheer entertainment it offered. The small, quiet Steventon society was enlarged and amplified by beings who were both like and unlike themselves. As a child, Jane Austen would have participated in family readings or, at the very least, would have found the latest novels displayed in her parents' parlor, many of them acquired from a circulating library in nearby Basingstoke. Her father was not inclined toward the role of censor, or perhaps he was preoccupied; in any case, he allowed his daughter to read what she liked. She loved, especially, the work of Samuel Richardson, and particularly a novel titled *The History of Sir Charles Grandison,* a seven-volume tome—one million words—which is little read today, a grand narrative excursion touching on adultery, drunkenness, rape, eroticism, fortune hunting, and most interestingly, the psychological effect of parents on their children—all of which seem a strong dose of worldliness for a rather protected young clergyman's daughter who nevertheless swallowed it down eagerly, making herself familiar with each scene, and perhaps thinking of it as a kind of fantasy rather than an imprint of the world's "reality." (Vladimir

Nabokov once remarked that "reality" was the one word in the English language that *always* needs a set of quotation marks around it.)

The pomposity and didacticism of *Sir Charles Grandison* cannot have escaped her, and she would have been provoked to laughter by Richardson's melodramatic effects. If we grant Jane Austen the least degree of prescience, we may be able to perceive her reading *against* the Richardson tradition, and unconsciously forming her own idea of the "realistic" novel and of what material she might herself include when her time came. She carried the Richardson influence throughout her writing life, but substituted wit for long-windedness and comedy for sententiousness. Turning away from Richardson's melodramatic excess, she trimmed and tempered her own episodes, and made certain they stood on legs that were psychologically sound. In Jane Austen's work there are no creatures resembling Richardson's thundering villain, Sir Hargrave Pollexfen, but instead the merely weak of heart: Wickham in *Pride and Prejudice* or Willoughby in *Sense and Sensibility* or the somewhat feckless but good-hearted Frank Churchill in *Emma*. In Jane Austen's novels there are no fainting women such as Richardson's ridiculous heroine, Harriet Byron. Austen's women don't faint unless they have real reason to; Louisa in *Persuasion* gives way to unconsciousness only when she is genuinely injured jumping from the wall in Lyme. Jane Austen admired the Richardson range, the undoubted energy and invention of the work, but she was able to replace sensation with sense and to avoid the kind of exaggeration that threatens to undermine the whole project of fiction.

Jane Austen's oldest brother, James, had turned to poetry and essay writing, and edited, for a time, a weekly magazine known as *The Loiterer,* in which the whole family took a keen interest. It is not surprising then, given her family circumstances, that Jane, early in her teens, should try her hand at writing too. But it is the satirical form of her youthful writing that astonishes us today. We can only guess that parody was the family flavor, and that the Austens were proud citizens of a satirical age.

What makes a child of twelve or thirteen a satirist? (To call her a teenager is to dip a toe in contemporary presumption—the term had not yet been invented, and adolescence carried few of the cultural weights it does today—but we can guess that a passage of biological and intellectual awkwardness has always prevailed to some extent in the species, requiring society's tact and ultimately its forbearance.) Jane Austen had been nurtured, certainly, in a circle appreciative of burlesque. She was narratively gifted and able to provide the kind of pleasure that was valued by her immediate audience, but she was also a small presence in a large and gifted household. Her desire to claim the attention of her parents and siblings can be assumed. She gave them what they wanted, that which would make them laugh and marvel aloud at her cleverness. Without a doubt, she took her cue from her literary brothers, James and Henry, both satirists, giving support to the dictum that writers are as good as the audience they wish to capture.

She was also awakened by the contemporary romantic novel, being, as we know from her own *Northanger Abbey*, a reader of romances, the kind of unserious literature that was in her day placed in female hands. Maria Edgeworth and Charlotte Smith, though, were among her favorite novelists; they were both intelligent writers, prolific and popular, and their novels can be read even today with interest. Austen also read Dr. Johnson and William Cowper at an early age, and the famously uneven Fanny Burney, but most young women of her time were protected, not to say deflected, from serious works. Readers, however, have always had the power to disrupt the bland surfaces of pedestrian fiction and convert the fluff of romance to something more nourishing. ("If a book is well written, I always find it too short," Jane Austen said of a Charlotte Smith work.) A deliberate and inventive misreading may have led her toward her vision of what a novel could do and be when fortified with irony and structure.

In the three notebooks of writing that have come down from Jane Austen's teen years we find a strain of burlesque, absurdly broad at first, and then more and more seen to be refining itself. At thirteen she can be observed rejoicing in her self-created role, the sentimental female who mocks her own sentimentality, invoking clichés that poke their long fingers at the shallowness of clichés. Using the name Sophia Sentiment, she writes to *The Loiterer* in an explosion of mock ex-asperation: "Only conceive, in eight papers, not one senti-mental story about love and honour and all that." The "all that" is the telling phrase, for clearly the subtext is "all that rubbish," or, at another level, "all that matters." In a similar vein, she informs *The Loiterer* that, should they publish ro-mantic fiction, "your hero and heroine must possess a great deal of feeling, and have very pretty names." In her satirical story "Jack and Alice," she creates a country gentleman who foils the women who pursue him by setting up steel traps around his estate. "Cruel Charles," one of these women laments, "to wound the hearts and legs of all the fair." The in-congruous linking of hearts and legs, of great feeling and pretty names, shows Jane, the clever child, pulling the rug out from under her own clever feet. It is as though she can't, for lack of nerve, speak without immediately subverting her own expression, with a need to charm and also to shock. Don't take me too seriously, she seems to be saying to her in-timate audience, at least not yet.

What kind of child was she? A cousin, Philadelphia Wal-ter, meeting the twelve-year-old Jane for the first time, found her "whimsical and affected," and certainly not as charming as her sister, Cassandra. She was intelligent, we can be cer-tain, and perhaps smug, heedless and prim at the same time, and accustomed to praise from those who knew her best. At home she was not as compelled to temper her opinions, nor constrained to behave as an ordinary well-brought-up child—and we all have seen how such outspoken, precocious children are misunderstood once they stray beyond the family circle.

To read this girlish work today is to see Jane Austen in the sometimes painful process of educating herself to become a writer. Trying on different genres was a way of discovering who she was and the kind of material she could best handle. Her faith in her own inventiveness must have grown with each completed piece, and so did an increasing understanding of psychological realism. Her haphazard schooling and undirected reading left her uncentered, longing for the attention of others, but crying out for her own attention as well.

Her early writing was produced within protective circumstances, and it is no surprise that her efforts are full of family jokes and private references, some of them stinging. The family response to her deliberate outrageousness may be imagined: a rolling of the eyes and "There goes our Jane again!" An almost reckless need to turn the world upside down can be glimpsed in the very early work. Everything in these narratives is at odds. The cozy allusions to family happenings conflict violently with tales of elopement and murder. Extraordinary and shocking class inversions occur, an upstairs/downstairs comedic eye that disappears completely in her mature period, when she seems to have understood the truth that satire can never be used against the powerless; the reader looks in vain to find such clichés as the comical servant or country rustic in Austen's great novels.

On the other hand, sexual innuendos leap from her mock

History of England, completed just before her sixteenth birth-day. Murders are committed. Duels are fought. It might even be said that duality fueled the earliest Austen persona, a crude, unnuanced, heartless world of black and white. Though she had not yet found her true expression, she con-cerned herself from the beginning with the sins of preten-tiousness, pomposity, and sentimentality, a thematic line that established itself in all her work.

Amidst all this dramatic exaggeration, there is little that has the feel of deliberate experiment. As a girl, she was less interested in creating new genres than in subverting those that were already established, and she seems to have happily truncated work that was not going well, killing off the more tiresome villains with a stroke of her pen. The chapters of her "novels" are very short, many of them mere gestures. In hind-sight, we can see that her gifts, particularly her sense of com-edy, were developing. Although there is a restlessness in her rapid skipping from one genre to the next—tributes, mock memoirs, histories, mininovels, verse, drama—and an impa-tience with extended work, she was respectful enough of her early efforts to keep amending them as she grew into her twenties. The survival of these early works says a good deal about the regard in which they were held by the Austen fam-ily; this beloved scribbling child consciously set out to enter-tain her small audience, but she was taken by them with a surprising measure of seriousness. She was encouraged, was supplied with precious paper, was listened to and applauded.

The best of the works waver between farce and feeling, as

though this young writer were torn in three directions, wanting to amuse and also to move her audience, and driven to express what some have called the Cinderella fantasy, the apprehension that a child is, for some mysterious reason, superior to his or her parents. *Lesley Castle,* an epistolary novel written around Jane's sixteenth year, indicates an early ability to convey individual voices and to embark on what must have seemed daring directions. Its heroine, Charlotte Lutterell, is intelligent, witty, astringent. ("I have often felt myself extremely satirical," says Charlotte at one point.) The novel includes an adulterous affair, the abandonment of a baby, and a conversion to Roman Catholicism—which must have left her Church of England father blinking. These forays into vice and high drama may have alarmed Mr. and Mrs. Austen, but their expression seems to have been tolerated. Curiously enough, though, this child of an amiable, indulgent family almost always, in her early work, sketches parents who are either cruel or neglectful or determined in one way or another to thwart the sensitivities of their offspring. What can we make of this? It's possible she was rebelling against a reality that remains invisible to us. Or she may have been frantic to dramatize what seemed narratively inert and uninteresting. In her mature work the despotic parent is given a much more believable shading, becoming the merely silly or ambitious parent, or the parent who favors one child over the other. Almost always in these cases Austen champions the underappreciated child—Elizabeth Bennet, Fanny Price—and holds the misguided parents up to ridicule.

The gradual softening of the parodic edge can be traced in even her earliest work. Her assaults as she moved through her teens were more and more indirectly delivered. The management of dialogue, undeveloped in her early work, became her weapon, replacing the crude manipulations of a disconnected narrator. Undoubtedly the family dramatics in the barn helped establish her ear, which in the later books is perfected. When Mrs. Allen in *Northanger Abbey,* for instance, says that Miss Tilney "always wears white," we are handed an economical piece of loaded information by the very person for whom this declaration has meaning: Mrs. Allen, a silly but shrewd woman, knows that someone who "always wears white" has no need to worry about the cost of laundering; someone who wears white exclusively has also adopted an eccentricity that speaks of a certain daintiness, and also resolution and stubbornness of mind.

Two qualities distinguish Jane Austen's early work from the juvenilia of other writers. The works were public, at least in a limited sense, and they were part of a continuum. The unformed writer who produced *Lesley Castle* in her teens is the same Jane Austen who was writing *Pride and Prejudice* at the extraordinary age of twenty-one, a mere five years later.

None of the early writing we have on record hints at the secrecy and confessional desperation associated with young girls. Instead, all of the work appears to have been shared openly with family and friends. The erasure of the private self from Jane Austen's early work suggests a confusion concerning that self or else a want of permission from those around her. Her maturing sensibility must be read today through the scrim of an increasingly subtle voice as she attempted to close the gap between longing and belonging, between wanting to please herself and placate her audience. Her satirical thrust remains in the foreground, but becomes more and more her own intricate invention. Moving from *Lesley Castle* to the later *Catharine*, we see her growing attention to plausibility, to psychological realism, and to expository halftones that mitigate the earlier childish excess.

In a notebook Mr. Austen presented to the young Jane, he provided a title for its eventual contents: "Effusions of Fancy by a very Young Lady Consisting of Tales in a Style entirely new." In this highly compressed, carefully constructed dedication, Mr. Austen gestures toward all that characterized his daughter's early writing; he reminds her, and perhaps himself, of her extreme youth, her tendency toward effusion and fancifulness, and at the same time he recognizes her uniqueness of style, her novelty of approach. This literary daughter of his had more than ordinary promise.

The fatherly inscription is tender and knowing and without real mockery. It can only have encouraged Jane Austen to write more.

4

THE BUSY, BUSTLING LIFE of the Austens was changing.
The house, in fact, was emptying out, with the Austen brothers going off in their separate directions. Francis was in the
East Indies, pursuing what was to become a successful naval
career, and Charles, the youngest Austen, was following in
his footsteps. The charming Henry, Jane's favorite brother,
was studying at Oxford, and James was now curate in the vicarage at nearby Overton. And Edward (lucky Edward,
adopted by the wealthy Knight family) was beginning his life
as a landed gentleman and considering a most advantageous
marriage. Jane, at home with her parents and her sister Cassandra, must have found herself in a debilitating vacuum.
Was this to be her life then? Her brothers had entered the
public world, while she and Cassandra were confined to domestic preoccupations and small social forays in the immediate neighborhood.

Some years earlier James had written a telling prologue
to one of the family theatricals. Times have changed, pro-
claimed cousin Eliza, who read the piece at the performance.
Women had been oppressed in the past:

But thank our happier Stars, those times are o'er
And woman holds a second place no more.
Now forced to quit their long held usurpation,
These Men all wise, these "Lords of the Creation,"
To our superior sway themselves submit,
Slaves to our charms and vassals to our wit;
We can with ease their ev'ry sense beguile,
And melt their Resolution with a smile . . .

Jane had just turned eleven when she sat listening to this curious and playful statement of emancipation, which can also be viewed as a sop tossed to women in exchange for what had been taken from them. Women's power was locked up in their charm and wit, in their targeted, practiced smiles. And this putative power could only be manipulated through a man, one of those so-called "Lords of Creation."

It cannot have been a surprise to such an observant child as Jane Austen that this kind of limited sway was all she was going to be allowed in her life, particularly when she would probably have been aware of Mary Wollstonecraft's *A Vindication of the Rights of Woman*, published in 1792, and widely discussed everywhere, perhaps even in the Steventon vicarage, where it must have offered warning rather than encouragement. Her girlhood writing both supports this harsh truth about women's lives and chafes against it, and her mature work, too, can be read as a demonstration of submissive women and the wiles they use to get their way—their pointed courtesies, quiet words of reproof, or directed glances. At the same time, the novels show men and women to be equal in intellect and moral apprehension. This is a great paradox, and one that Jane Austen appears to have swallowed, but cannot have failed to notice.

The reality of her situation as she approached the age of twenty must have been shocking. She had no profession, and none would be offered to her. Governessing, school teaching–there was little else for women in her position, and she scorned both. She was without money of her own, except for £20 allowance a year from her father, and this dispensed in quarterly lumps. It has been suggested by the contemporary scholar Edward Copeland that we calculate a Jane Austen pound as being equivalent to $100 US dollars today, which allows Jane an annual budget of $2,000 out of the family budget of £600, or $60,000, a comfortable family income, but not at all luxurious–not when a circular mahogany dining table with strap hinges, for example, cost £5.7.6., or almost $600, and a backgammon table was priced at £1.10.0., which would be more than $100 today.

Jane Austen's visits away from home were arranged by others, and at their convenience rather than hers. She was, in fact, dependent on the good will of family and friends for all the requirements of life and must at times have imagined and projected herself forward into the pitiable state of a spinster, spooked even at this young age by the tiresome, embarrassing neediness of Miss Bates (*Emma*) or the determinedly cheerful Mrs. Smith (*Persuasion*) and their sadly disadvantaged sisters who populated novels, women trapped between social levels and prohibited by their precariously balanced intelligence from participation in active life. For them there were only the available tricks of charm and the plotted dramas of entrapment, the glance over the tea table that redirected action or else, with great kindness and cunning, drew men away from their paralyzed silence.

Meanwhile, at Steventon, she had her books, her pianoforte, and her needlework, an activity she seems to have taken seriously. And she had her writing, which from the ages of fifteen to seventeen engaged her fully. And she had her friends. Now that the family at home was dwindling, a small sitting room was set up for her sister and herself, and here they could entertain a circle of neighboring young women. With its chocolate carpet, its bookshelves and the pianoforte, the room must have seemed cramped but congenial. The work boxes of the two sisters were displayed, and probably Cassandra's watercolors, too, and Jane's writing desk, the emblems of their particular expression. New neighbors, the Lloyds, arrived in the district in 1789, and Jane became fast friends with Martha Lloyd, who, though she was ten years older, possessed a similarly animated spirit. The Bigg-Wither family, with three daughters, settled in a nearby manor house. The society of these new companions was diverting and congenial. Girlish talk held sway: clothes, books, dance steps, neighborhood gossip; giddy expeditions were planned: long walks or trips into Basingstoke. (These female relationships were important to Jane Austen, whose novels ring with the music of high spirits and feminine laughter.) By the age of seventeen she was attending local balls and becoming a practiced flirt. The writer Mary Russell Mitford described her unkindly as "the prettiest, silliest, most affected husband-hunting butterfly she ever remembered." But where was all this leading?

The dramatic story of Jane Austen's French relations, Aunt Philadelphia and her daughter Eliza, had always been present as a parallel strand in her life, as complex and filled with mystery and color as the most potent novel. Enough years had passed to melt the early part of the account into near legend. Philadelphia Austen, the sister of George Austen, had traveled alone to India in 1752, seeing that her only chance for a life was to find a rich husband. The ensuing marriage to the much older Tysoe Saul Hancock was not a happy one, and Philadelphia's only daughter, Eliza, was probably fathered by the more dashing Warren Hastings, governor-general of India. Eliza, a lifelong friend of Jane Austen, grew up to marry Jean Capot, Comte de Feuillide, an ambitious French entrepreneur who was guillotined in the bloody years following the French Revolution. A widow and the mother of a son, Eliza later married Henry Austen, Jane's much adored brother, and became Jane's sister-in-law.

This particular family narrative–Philadelphia the bold adventurer and her daughter Eliza–must have dazzled young Jane Austen with its romance and its international dimensions, and it is impossible to contemplate Austen's life without taking so large a connection into account. From early childhood she knew she possessed an aunt who had risked everything at the age of twenty-two to go out to India, into unknown territory, where she re-created herself and her possibilities. Eliza's history is equally dramatic–uncertain parentage, a marriage into French nobility, danger, tragedy, and finally a triumph of courage and a dash to safety within the embrace of the Austen family.

There was much visiting and letter writing between the two families after the return from India, and there can be no doubt that Jane Austen's imagination was stirred by the story of her aunt and cousin. We see a flicker of this kind of glamorized history and worldly intrigue in a girlhood work, *Love and Friendship* (dedicated to Eliza), in which one of the characters, Laura, gives a breezy account of her life:

My father was a native of Ireland and an inhabitant of Wales; My Mother was the natural Daughter of a Scotch Peer by an Italian Opera-girl–I was born in Spain and received my Education at a Convent in France.

There is such a strong yearning for the exotic in this passage, such subversion of class and order! Jane Austen, bent over her needlework in the quiet of an English country rectory, was alive to the drama of her own extended family history and to her own unmet longings. Other women–family members, her own aunt and cousin–had seized their opportunities, risked their respectability, and claimed their future. What was she herself doing, other than scribbling away for the entertainment of the family and waiting for a husband to appear? And from where would that husband come? Candidates were sure to be in short supply, since neither of the Austen girls had a penny to bring to marriage, but still Jane dreamed of rescue. Once, idly, she covered a page of her father's parish ledger with the names of fantasy husbands: "Henry Frederick Howard Fitzwilliam," "Edmund Arthur William Mortimer." These were noble-sounding gentlemen with a ring of fortune about them. Then, out of a different longing, or perhaps terror, she wrote "Jack Smith," to be married to "Jane Smith late Austen."

Her life went on quietly. There were pleasant diversions, holidays with the family, visits from Eliza and her son, and preparations for the wedding of the Austen cousin, Jane Cooper. The officiating clergyman at this event was to be the handsome young Tom Fowle, whose family were old friends of the Austens and who had himself been a pupil in Mr. Austen's rectory school. It was during this prewedding period that Tom and Cassandra became engaged.

Much of what we know about the relationship between the two Austen sisters derives from their correspondence, those periods during which they were separated. A letter, even to an intimate, brings another self forward, one that is more formalized and detached or else heightened and exaggerated. The letter writer's persona is constructed and brought to artificial life, and there is in Jane Austen's letters to her sister a witty, distracted performer at work, and one who longs to shorten the distance between herself and Cassandra by sharing the minutiae of daily life.

Their day-to-day relationship can only be guessed at,

though Mrs. Austen is famous for saying that if Cassandra should cut off her head, so too would Jane. Quiet days spent together as they approached maturity are largely undescribed, and we tend to think of them as without event. Which is why the engagement of Cassandra comes with something of a thud in any account of Jane Austen's life–we know so little about what led up to it, how it came to be.

And we can't be sure what seventeen-year-old Jane thought about her only sister's engagement. We do know that she composed for Cassandra a darkly romantic poem titled "Ode to Pity," which fell rather short as a statement of sisterly rejoicing.

> Ever musing, I delight to tread
>> The paths of honour and the myrtle grove
> Whilst the pale Moon her beams doth shed
>> On disappointed love.

Disappointed love? Whatever could she have meant? She also dispatched oddly worded messages of greeting to her newly born nieces, Anna and Fanny, the daughters of her brothers James and Edward; these missives were meant, perhaps, to be ironic, but the tone is heavy, almost bitter. Once again Jane Austen may have glimpsed the emptiness of the future. Her brothers were marrying and having children, and now her sister would be leaving home. She was relieved, probably, when the young couple, both of them penniless, postponed their marriage until Tom was on firmer financial ground. In the meanwhile he accepted a post as chaplain to a regiment headed in late 1795 for the West Indies, and the possibility of combat with the French.

Jane Austen's writing output slowed down somewhat in her late teens when she seems to have been too occupied with the real business of romance and flirtation to spin mere fictions. But then, all at once, when she was about twenty, she completed a short novel, *Lady Susan.* Her father had given her a portable writing desk for her nineteenth birthday, a pretty thing of mahogany and leather, equipped with a glass inkstand and a drawer. The gift may have represented a kind of permission on her parent's part, exactly what all young writers need if they are to continue in their pursuit. Or it may have been a suggestion—fatherly, kindly—that she distract herself by attention to her desk rather than to the wild flirting he had witnessed or heard about at recent balls. *Lady Susan* was the first piece she wrote at this new desk.

Her brothers, during this period, were engaged in combat at sea while she, at home at Steventon, pen in hand, brought to the page the only kind of combat a woman was allowed: the conquest of hearts and the overturning of domestic arrangements. The novel, never published during her lifetime, is her strangest and most unsettling literary offering and seems to have been unpopular with her family and friends. It is charmless. And very nearly pointless. Its form—a novel in letters—is not one that suited Jane Austen, whose own correspondence was familial and unfocused, with only occasional bursts of sparkle. She knew how to write a polite formal note, but in her letters to Cassandra she adopted early on a flighty, breathless persona, determinedly unserious and even appeasing, as though pleasing Cassandra, amusing Cassandra, was all that guided her pen. The plot of *Lady Susan* is very much off-the-shelf for its time: A wicked mother attempts to force her daughter into an unwanted marriage. Lady Susan is manipulative, cruel and selfish, abusive to her child, and traitorous to her friends, a predatory female of almost monstrous size. Her original marriage schemes are confounded, but she shows not the slightest degree of shame or self-awareness as a reader might have expected by the novel's end, and Jane Austen does not mete out to her what would be an appropriate punishment. It may be that Austen half admired her creation's mixture of cunning and sexual bravura; Lady Susan was at least capable of exercising power—even though this force was chiefly directed at breaking up homes and managing her daughter's misery. The corrupt heart of Lady Susan gestures backward toward the juvenilia; Lady Susan's lack of moral judgment looks ahead to Mary Crawford in *Mansfield Park* or even to the flawed Emma.

Jane Austen may have been merely "trying her hand" at a popular form in the same way that contemporary novelists sometimes take a flyer at a romance novel. She may have been touched by *Les Liaisons Dangereuses,* which was widely known at the time. Or perhaps she was teaching herself a new expressiveness; the materials of *Lady Susan* are flimsy, but the knit is tight. She had learned while writing *Lady Susan* about the novelist's control. And she was soon to try something a good deal more ambitious.

5

In 1795, just twenty years old, Jane Austen began a new epistolary novel about two sisters, Elinor and Marianne, who, like the Austen sisters, are without money and each of them longing for marriage. The two characters differ sharply in temperament. Marianne, the impulsive, swooning, impractical younger sister, is allied by her nature to the forces of true love and happiness. Elinor, the older sister, is on the side of prudence—acquiescence is closer to the mark—and modestly in love with an equally prudent young man whose family is totally opposed to a match with such an impecunious family. At this, Elinor can only shrug her agreement; she perfectly understands the importance of money and station, as Marianne does not. Jane Austen, writing to Cassandra, who was visiting her fiancé's family at the time, allied herself with Marianne: "I write only for fame," she said, "and without any view to pecuniary emolument."

It is impossible to read this declaration without hearing a harsh note of self-mockery; the mention of the word "fame" by someone as unknown and isolated as the young Jane Austen requires an arch, undercutting tone that Cassandra would be able to interpret without the least hesitation. She might also understand, as a contemporary reader of the letters does, that there is a sense in which Jane Austen meant what she said: She hungered for fame and may have felt, even at this stage of her development, deserving of it, knowing at the same time that such a yearning could not be expressed in anything other than an ironic voice. Her new effort, *Elinor and Marianne,* her longest novel yet, might just possibly serve as her introduction to the world. We know it as an early draft of *Sense and Sensibility.*

The manuscript was read to the family, although not one page of it has come down to us today. We recognize those familiar names and register the subject: two sisters of fundamentally different character searching for love and happiness, each in thrall to their very different loves. The novel is saved from the simplicity of allegory by the fact that Marianne's sensibility and Elinor's sense are not perfectly idealized or opposed; they are, each of them, a little silly and a little calculating. We have real sisters here, and not convenient contrarieties. Their devotion to each other pulls the novel's sometimes tenuous structure tight.

But the embryo novel must have had a very different trajectory. An epistolary novel can only exist if its characters are separated from each other and obliged to correspond–this artificial construct is one of the problems with the novel-in-letters. In *Sense and Sensibility,* which abandoned the epistolary form for a third-person narrative, the two sisters are scarcely ever apart.

And something else intervened in the life of Jane Austen

soon after she finished *Marianne and Elinor* and was perhaps considering a revised narrative approach: She fell in love, or at least what she took for a form of love.

There is a joke among novelists that in order to initiate strong action or to revive a wilting narrative it is only necessary to say: "And so a stranger came to town." The arrival of a stranger, in fact, was the spark that ignited, and perhaps changed forever, the developing sensibility of Jane Austen.

It was January of the year 1796. Jane had just turned twenty. The stranger was Tom Lefroy, from Ireland, visiting relations at nearby Ashe parsonage before beginning his law studies in London. He was young, pleasant, good-looking, and had already taken a degree in Dublin. (All the heroes of Jane Austen's mature novels are reading men, men of the book, and clever Tom Lefroy is no exception.) He and Jane Austen met only a few times, but they seemed to enjoy the same high spirits and sense of irony. Jane's letters to Cassandra at this time show her to be thoroughly smitten, unable to restrain herself from repeated references to her "Irish friend." Her spirits are effervescent as she reports on an evening spent with him at a local ball. "Imagine to yourself," she confides boldly, "everything most profligate and shocking in the way of dancing and sitting down together." As usual, she cushions her enthusiasm with one of her typical throwaway gestures, claiming that Tom Lefroy's one fault was that "his morning coat is a great deal too light," and clearly she intended to correct this fault in exactly the lighthearted way by which women were permitted to bring men to a state of ex-

cellence. Tom Lefroy calls on her after the evening of "profligate" behavior, and their open discussion of the novel *Tom
Jones* gives a sense of the ease they felt together, for the response of shock to the bawdiness of *Tom Jones* had not diminished since its publication. That two young people could
discuss such a work suggests a willingness to go beyond flirtation into an area of sensuous exploration. She was keenly
conscious of his being teased for his attentions to her, as she
wrote to Cassandra, and she expected the drama to play itself out at the next ball—"I rather expect to receive an offer
from my friend in the course of the evening. I shall refuse
him, however, unless he promises to give away his white
Coat."

It did not happen. She was snatched from the good novel
she had imagined herself into and placed into an alternate
narrative of class bitterness. The real world that her heroine
Elinor had recognized had intervened, the world of money
and practical considerations, and the hero, it turned out, was
part of a pragmatic design. For Jane Austen's Tom Lefroy
was gone, swiftly removed by the Lefroy family, who had
greater plans for this young man than marriage to an un-
moneyed clergyman's daughter who would not be allowed,
after all, to utter a lighthearted acceptance of marriage, un-
dercut only by the condition of the white coat.

She never saw him again, although it is clear she thought
of him. It is also apparent that the episode multiplied itself
again and again in her novels, embedded in the theme of
thwarted love and loss of nerve. In the novels, happily, there

is often a second or third chance, a triumphant overriding of class difference, but between Jane Austen and Tom Lefroy there is only silence. He returned to Ireland after his studies, married an heiress, produced a large family, became something of a pious bore, and eventually rose to become chief justice of Ireland.

She responded to her heartbreak with typical self-mockery, turning herself for a brief time into the role of abandoned lover, overflowing tears and all. Friends rushed to comfort her, but the experience must have been genuinely humiliating, especially since she had broadcast her hopes to Cassandra. Had she foolishly magnified a relationship that was barely in its infancy—three or four balls and one visit to Steventon, some shared laughter and literary exchanges, and perhaps a kiss or two? Certainly she had misjudged the threat she posed to the Lefroy family.

The romantic impulse that had accompanied her since her early youth fell at least partly away. She was no longer a child passionate about the certainty of love overcoming all obstacles. She was an unmarried woman of twenty who, because of her lack of fortune, was going to have fewer and fewer choices. Like Elinor, like Marianne, her two new heroines, she was vulnerable to a society she was just beginning to understand.

She buried herself in gossip, in family doings, in a prolonged visit to her brother Edward's family in Kent, but her greatest comfort may have come from her ebullient London cousin, Eliza. The two of them carried on a lively correspondence and saw each other as frequently as possible. Eliza, two years a widow, was a vivid presence, a woman of affairs who managed to keep the romantic flame alive in a pragmatic world. Already she was looking around and assessing her chances of forming new attachments, but she was in no hurry. Marriage could be a form of subjugation, she believed. There might be other possibilities for women of wit and intelligence.

6

TOM FOWLE WAS DEAD. The shocking news arrived at Steventon from the West Indies in the spring of 1797. Cassandra's beloved fiancé had perished of yellow fever and been buried at sea. An Easter wedding had been planned and then postponed when Tom failed to return. The Austen family was in deep mourning. From all reports, Cassandra Austen's behavior took the form of dignified stoicism, and even though she was in her early twenties she seems to have withdrawn almost at once into a life of quiet spinsterhood, or even a sort of symbolic widowhood. Prudent young Tom Fowle had taken the precaution of making a will before he set out, leaving Cassandra with a sum of £1,000. Close to being a widow's inheritance, it was not enough to live on but enough to make her, for the rest of her life, somewhat less dependent on family funds. A young woman of vigor and humor–her sister Jane once called her "the finest comic writer of the present age"–she entered at age twenty-four a premature middle age, assuming some of her mother's domestic burdens and transforming herself into a devoted maiden aunt. The two sisters clung together in their numb sorrow, or so it seemed to their friends, their lives more closely entwined than ever before. "They alone fully understood what each had suffered and felt and thought," one family member recounted.

And yet, all around them life was going on. Cousin Eliza stepped into the inner circle of the Austen family with a dramatic double flourish. First she refused James Austen's offer of marriage (James's wife, Anne, had died early in his marriage), and then, in 1797, she and Henry Austen, ten years her junior, were married. It was a marriage useful to both in practical terms and also, it appears, an affair of passion that lasted until Eliza's death in 1813.

Inevitably Jane Austen was spun into her own family chronicle of grief and consolation. At the same time she was hard at work on a new novel she titled, provisionally, *First Impressions,* which was really about the *faultiness* of first impressions, or how an intelligent young woman named Elizabeth Bennet forms an entrenched negative opinion of an arrogant young man, Darcy, whom she believes has insulted herself and her family.

Jane Austen, unlike her sister, had not given up her own delight in balls and flirtations, though her hopes at this time seem to have been growing dimmer. The Lefroy family, perhaps to make amends for the Tom Lefroy debacle, attempted a piece of heavy matchmaking with a young clergyman, Samuel Blackall, but between Blackall and Jane there existed a cloud of mutual indifference. She sensed, humiliatingly, that she was not noticeably sought after at balls, writing to

Cassandra, "I do not think I am very much in request–People are rather apt not to ask me till they could not help it . . ."

As *First Impressions* took shape, the Austen family, those eager aficionados of the novel, followed the fortunes of Jane Bennet and Mr. Bingley, of Elizabeth and Darcy, as though they were real people, neighbors whose entanglements and betrayals touched each of them. Mr. Collins, perhaps the most fully comic of the Austen characters (and possibly modeled on Samuel Blackall), moved into Steventon with his obsequies and absurdities and lack of sense, providing welcome laughter in a bleak season.

It is sometimes thought that the Austen novels are dense and slow moving. The opposite is true, as her readers know. She mastered, early on, the ability to move scenes briskly along. Moments of perceived inaction contrast sharply with abrupt psychological shifts. Always there is the sense that she knows where she's going, even in the midst of digression. This assured narrative voice anchors and sustains the human drama, and it is a particular pleasure for the reader to find important moments buried in paragraphs that pretend to be flattened asides.

First Impressions, much later renamed *Pride and Prejudice,* turned on the human capacity to judge–or to misjudge–the difference between appearance and reality. Was Darcy ever as disdainful and distant as Elizabeth believed, or did a girlish longing for drama–a drama in which she is the self-selected heroine–exaggerate her response to him and distort her initial impression? She certainly has doubts about her own judgment following Darcy's first and unanticipated declaration of love. Immediately after, when she finds herself alone, she sits down and cries for half an hour. The crisp precision of that half-hour bawl is typically Elizabeth and typical of Jane Austen, too. A fifteen-minute howl would show lack of sensibility and a full hour, lack of sense. Weeping, in Elizabeth's case, gives way to "agitated reflections," and by the next morning she turns, sensibly, to the remedy of "air and exercise" and to a serious rethinking about Mr. Darcy's motives.

Elizabeth Bennet is a brilliantly drawn and attractive character, and the novel is so subtly paced that even after repeated readings readers find themselves growing tense as the story progresses, preparing for disappointment, fearing that Elizabeth has gone too far this time, that she has, through pride, through rigidity of mind, lost the one person capable of rescuing her and giving her the life she deserves.

It is difficult to love Darcy, though readers are attracted to something glittering and hard in his personality. There is always a sense that he is behaving with a little too much dignity, that he is in some sense doing Elizabeth a favor by falling in love with her, acting against his best instincts and caving in to a fatal male weakness, sacrificing himself however nobly, and paying altogether too much attention to the shallow, spiteful Bingley sisters.

The "voice" of the novel is not delivered with the mature Austen measure, but is instead a cry of youthful anguish, the acknowledgment that one's parents often present an acute embarrassment. The silly are allowed to lead the sensible into peril. And parents are capable of separating their children from their destinies, simply by being parents: blockish, awkward, old-fashioned, countrified, and coarse. In novel after novel the Austen pattern is replayed, the non-Darwinian emergence of brilliance from a dull dynasty: Elizabeth Bennet's ravishing intelligence, Fanny Price's perfect balance, Anne Elliot's assurance and sense of self—all these women overthrow the throttled lives they are born into and the oafish parents who bring them into the world and then leave them adrift. There is a sense in which Jane Austen wrote not so much about marriage as about the tension between parents and children, the inevitable rupture between generations and the destruction that carelessness and inattention to these bonds can bring about. We are led inevitably back to the question of her own parents, and the glazed cleverness, and perhaps care, with which she covered the Austen biographical tracks.

Because her bright, splintery dialogue is so often interrupted by a sad, unanswerable tone of estranged sympathy, stirred by complacent acts of hypocrisy or injustice, the reader of Austen's novels comes again and again to the reality of a ferocious and persistent moral anger. It is a manageable anger, and artfully concealed by the mechanism of an arch, incontrovertible amiability. Even her own family, her close circle of readers, may have missed the astringency of her observations.

Her own reading had comprised sentimental novels and

novels of terror. These models must have disappointed her in some way, failing in their connection to the life she knew existed and proving incapable of illuminating the subtle shifts of feeling between people as they came to know each other. Probably she found the novels she read just a little absurd, and for a time she was able to rejoice in the humor and horror they provided. It was their exaggeration that made them absurd, but the real absurdity lay in their preoccupations, the strangeness of the human dilemmas on the page. What she wanted, and what she accomplished, was the dramatization of the familiar, the recognizable; and though *Pride and Prejudice* is closer to being a romance than any of her other novels, it takes as its subject the very issue that Jane Austen was struggling with at the age of twenty-one. Human beings required love and location, but society, with its sharp class separations, stood in the way of a woman's fulfillment. The novel, in its subject, is both like and different from her own circumstances, and its ebullience convinces the reader of Austen's own enjoyment of the mingled episodes of comedy and longing. Physicality and youth push the story toward its fairy-tale denouement. The young Bennet sisters are healthy, vital creatures, and the men–Bingley, Darcy, Wickham– burst with male strength and attractiveness.

Elizabeth looks for a time to have lost her chance at happiness. She has refused Mr. Collins and also Darcy, and has lost Wickham to her sister Lydia. Despite this, she remains surprisingly sanguine, convinced as she is of her essential worth. Her confrontation with Lady Catherine is one of the most vigorous and triumphant scenes in literature, for here she is allowed the full honesty we know her to possess. She is reckless; she is morally certain of her ground, and she understands despite her youth just what is at stake.

Mr. Austen, Jane's father, was an inveterate reader of comic novels, and he clearly saw, even beyond a father's natural fond inclination, that *First Impressions* was publishable. In November 1797 he picked up his pen and wrote to the publisher Thomas Cadell in London.

"I have in my possession a manuscript novel, comprised in three vols about the length of Miss Burney's *Evelina*. As I am well aware of what consequence it is that a work of this sort should make its first appearance under a respectable name, I apply to you. Shall be much obliged therefore if you will inform me whether you chuse to be concerned in it. What will be the expense of publishing at the author's risk; & what will you venture to advance for the property of it, if on a perusal, it is approved of? Should your answer give me encouragement I will send you the work."

Even knowing that Mr. Austen was not in the habit of writing such flogging letters, we marvel today at how restrained his words are when compared with today's covering letter to a book publisher. He is concerned, it seems, mainly with the financing of the venture. He is utterly circumspect about the author, who she might be, what his relationship to her is. He says nothing at all about the subject of the novel, and not one word about the vibrancy of the writing. He does, on the other hand, and perhaps too openly, flatter the publisher with his "respectable name," and he attempts to enhance the novel's appeal by a sideways reference to *Evelina*. Here he very likely misjudged the effect; Fanny Burney's novel had been published almost twenty years earlier and was written in a style that by the end of the eighteenth century was decidedly dated.

In any case, Mr. Austen's letter of inquiry did not stir any interest at all at Thomas Cadell's office. Someone wrote across the top of the page: "declined by return of post."

We have no way of knowing how this rejection was received at Steventon. Mr. Austen, who seems not to have pursued the matter with other publishers, was undoubtedly disappointed that he was not to have some relief from a steadily dwindling income. He was no longer taking pupils, his farm income was unreliable, and it appeared more and more likely that his two daughters were not going to make brilliantly advantageous marriages or, in fact, any kind of marriage at all.

Did Jane Austen know that her father had approached a publisher, and if so, was she crushed by the publisher's lack of interest? We know only that she turned her energies, and perhaps her disappointment, toward a revision of her earlier work, *Elinor and Marianne*, which she had renamed *Sense and Sensibility*. She was entering a period of growing confidence in her abilities, and this new assurance must have defended her against the casual dismissal, the cruelty of the phrase "declined by return of post." Her reworking of earlier texts suggests a new ease with the form and direction of her work—which was immediate and as close to her as her needlework and her daily engagement with the pianoforte. The world of London publishers, on the other hand, was distant, and chances of publication remote. Meanwhile, she had her small audience: her family, a few friends. And she had, it would seem, a gathering of faith in her own work. She must have known, as the old century was drawing to a close, exactly how good a writer she really was.

7

ALL HER LIFE Jane Austen inhabited the world of the lesser gentility with its necessary thrift. Her letters, and her novels too, show a very real concern with the cost of articles. She knew the monetary value of a yard of good wool cloth or a basket of apples. There were always servants in the Austen household, but they were few in number, and the Austen women themselves augmented their efforts, supervising meals, ordering supplies, mending and remaking garments, and sewing the shirts that the men of the family wore. Many of their neighbors lived in far grander circumstances, but the Austen family, with their church and family connections, were respected and made welcome. They were recommended, also, by the fact that they were better educated than many they came face to face with, so that their wit, their liveliness, and their conversation leveled some of the barriers that lack of wealth might place in the way.

It was through her brother Edward that Jane Austen was exposed to the very different realm of great wealth and ease. Edward's adoption by the Knight family had cast him into the role of landed gentleman, and as a young woman Jane made many visits to Kent, where Edward and his family lived, first at the relatively modest house Rowling, and later at the great family seat of Godmersham. The eighteenth-century dwelling, still standing today, is set in the midst of a private landscaped park. Its marble-floored foyer is beautifully proportioned, and gives way to large, airy reception rooms, including a library where Jane Austen once found herself alone during a visit, musing on the presence of twenty-eight chairs, five tables, and *two* fires. Her gleeful counting of those twenty-eight chairs tells us something about how she regarded such wealth—as utterly delightful, something to be enjoyed and luxuriated in, and also more than a little bit foolish.

She was, over the years, less a guest at Godmersham than a relation who was sent for in time of need, helping to look after Edward's very large family and to assist his wife, Elizabeth, when a new baby was due to arrive. Jane must have looked carefully, with a sly and intense regard, at everyday life in a great house. When she later wrote, through the thoughts of Elizabeth Bennet, that "to be mistress of Pemberley might be something!" it is with the full force of admiration for the power of land ownership and a wistful longing for the luxury that attends it. There is an air—coming as it does from Jane Austen, and from the morally fastidious Elizabeth Bennet—just a little vague and unspecified about that word "something," and we have to let it fall on our ears with all its tones of stunning surprise and exuberance, and certainly a measure of confusion about what material possessions could bring.

Jane Austen's satirical powers would have been stirred by the exuberant culture of the newly rich, and everything we know about her tells us she would not necessarily have hidden her response. Elizabeth, Edward's wife, was not fond of her clever sister-in-law, preferring Cassandra, and she made that distinction clear, although Edward's adopted mother, Mrs. Knight, always treated Jane with kindness and respect.

Probably Austen never got over the sense of being the poor visiting sister. Her favorite niece, Fanny, recalled many years later what Aunt Jane was like. This recollection was put down in 1869, almost fifty years after Jane Austen's death, when Fanny was an elderly woman writing to a younger sister who would not have remembered her aunt's visits.

> Yes my love it is very true that Aunt Jane from various circumstances was not so *refined* as she ought to have been from her *talent*, & if she had lived 50 years later she would have been in many respects more suitable to *our* more refined tastes. They were not rich & the people around with whom they chiefly mixed, were not at all high bred, or in short anything more than mediocre & *they* of course tho' superior in *mental powers & cultivation* were on the same level so far as *refinement* goes—but I think in later life their intercourse with Mrs. Knight (who was very fond of & kind to them) improved them both & Aunt Jane was too clever not to put aside all possible signs of "common-ness" (if such an expression is allowable) & teach herself to be more refined, at least in intercourse with people in general.

Both the Aunts (Cassandra & Jane) were brought up in the most complete ignorance of the World & its ways (I mean as to fashion &c) & if it had not been for Papa's marriage which brought them into Kent & the kindness of Mrs. Knight, who used often to have one or the other of the sisters staying with her, they would have been, tho' not less clever & agreeable in themselves, very much below par as to good society & its ways. If you hate all this I beg yr. Pardon, but I felt it at my *pen's end,* & it chose to come along & speak the truth.

The letter, so cozily couched, stings the heart. It is a measure of the affection in which Jane Austen's readers hold her, that they are almost always offended by the tone and contents of this letter. The snobbery, the casual disregard, the disloyalty of a beloved niece—all this seems intolerable, even though Jane Austen was perfectly capable of writing blunt letters herself. Perhaps Fanny in her old age had forgotten what her aunt was really like, giving way to an accretion of images that surround departed family members, especially those who have achieved a degree of recognition that surprises and shocks succeeding generations. It may be—there are signs—that Fanny was on the brink of dementia. Or perhaps—and this has to be taken into account—there is a measure of truth at the bottom of her assessment.

What exactly is refinement? And in what might Jane Austen's presumed lack of refinement lie? Her clothes would have been simpler and fewer than those worn by her brother

Edward's family and friends: During this period wealthy women changed their dress several times a day, a habit that would have been impossible for the Austen sisters. She had country rather than town manners and valued openness over concealment and sense over sentimentality. Her familiarity with servants might have been differently gauged. Her use of language may have been sharper, more direct, lacking the extravagant locutions and fashionable references of Edward's circle. She lived, it might almost be said, in a different England, a simpler time, before the elaborate courtesies and distinctions of the Victorian age had come to flower. She was used to dining in the midafternoon, not at the newly fashionable hour of half past six. And life at Godmersham, its abundance and wastefulness, may have stimulated in her behavior psychological defenses that were interpreted as antisocial.

Refinement is relative, of course. Jane Austen once wrote to Cassandra about some acquaintances, how "they do not know how *to be particular*" (her italics), meaning that some lapse of courtesy had been committed, some social roughness of manner displayed. We know she was given to careful distinctions of behavior, writing about Mrs. Armstrong, the mother of an acquaintance in Lyme Regis, who "sat darning a pr of Stockings the whole of my visit . . ." This breach of etiquette, similar perhaps to pulling out one's knitting at a contemporary dinner party, showed a hostess's unwillingness to devote complete attention to a guest, preferring to get on with more immediate and practical tasks.

Aunt Jane once wrote that she considered the young Fanny to be "almost another sister" and "quite after one's own heart," which makes the "Yes my love" letter particularly bitter. Fanny's word "mediocre" is especially cruel, and more so because we know that Fanny appreciated her aunt's genius. And yet, Jane Austen *was* eccentric to her time. Another niece, Marianne Knight, remembers how her aunt, working quietly by the fire at Godmersham, would mysteriously burst into laughter and hurry across the room to write something down, then return to her place. Unexplained laughter, erratic movement—these would have been enough in an age of highly codified behavior to raise concern about Aunt Jane's lack of refinement.

Undoubtedly Jane Austen benefited from her visits to Kent, a place, she once wrote with sweeping exaggeration, where everyone is rich. A social window was opened to her, and it was one she could make ready use of in her writing. Nonetheless, there are those who believe that her poor-relative status and the suffering this caused her may have injured her self-regard and contributed to a gathering sense of bitterness. Without a doubt she was condescended to. The hairdresser who came to prepare the Godmersham ladies for an evening party offered the visiting Jane Austen a discount, recognizing her at once as a poor relation, someone to be pitied and accommodated. We know that during one prolonged stay at Godmersham, she expressed in the most piercing tones a longing for home, for the simplicity of Steventon (and later Chawton), with its opportunity for open conversation and simple routines, and for the dependable, satisfying companionship of her sister and mother and a few agreeable neighbors.

Probably she came to believe that the two worlds—wealthy Kent and familiar, humble Hampshire—were irreconcilable. She belonged to one and not to the other. There may well have been pain in exclusion and humiliation, but there was always the pleasure of going home, to the place where she knew she would be welcomed.

8

WE THINK OF *Pride and Prejudice* as Jane Austen's sunniest novel, and yet it was written during a period of unhappiness. No letters survive from the year 1797, and this is a clue, though an unreliable one. Cassandra, we know, was recovering from the death of her fiancé, and Jane from her disappointment over Tom Lefroy. The household at Steventon had shrunk. Visitors continued to arrive, but the ongoing bustle of life in the country rectory had faded. Probably there was less noise, less laughter. Theatricals in the barn were a thing of the past. The Austen parents were growing older, and finances, too, were thinner.

Yet from this difficult time sprang a fast-paced, exuberant, much loved novel with a new kind of heroine, a young woman of warmth and intelligence who, by the flex of her own mind, remakes her future and makes it spectacularly. The detachment of Jane Austen's imaginative flight from her personal concerns is extraordinary, even given the fiction writer's license. *Pride and Prejudice* can be seen as a palimpsest, with Jane Austen's real life engraved roughly, enigmatically, beneath its surface. Elizabeth Bennet, like Jane Austen, is in her early twenties and has an older sister, Jane, whom she adores. Jane and Elizabeth's parents share a problem with the Austen parents: how to find husbands for daughters of small fortune. Elizabeth also has Jane Austen's quickness of mind, but she is not Jane Austen. The Bennet household is more comfortable, less isolated, and employs a larger number of servants. Elizabeth's Longbourn is not Steventon, and agriculture is not a felt presence. Mr. Bennet, unlike the Reverend George Austen, has no profession. The Bennet family members are more seriously divided in their interests and in their characters than the Austens. It is less possible to imagine them, for example, merging their energies and putting on a play for one another's entertainment. Their conversation never achieves the Austen elegance and erudition. Their social awkwardness, partly because of Mrs. Bennet's risible nature and Mr. Bennet's morose obstinacy, is an exaggeration of the Austens' unease.

Where then did Jane Austen find the material for her novel? Every writer draws on his or her own experience; where else could the surface details of a novel's structure come from, especially a novel as assured in its texture as *Pride and Prejudice*? But it is not every novelist's tactic to draw *directly* on personal narrative, and Jane Austen, clearly, is not a writer who touches close to the autobiographical core. There is, famously, the gift of an amber cross from her brother Charles and its fictional translation, in which it becomes the topaz cross Fanny Price in *Mansfield Park* is given by her brother William. But this is a mere narrative point, not a whole narrative parcel. Some readers have found a resemblance between the fictional Mr. Collins and the real Samuel Blackall, but so little is known about Mr. Blackall that the likeness remains pure conjecture. It is also suggested that the wicked, ruthless Lady Susan is drawn from stories about a wicked Lady Craven, the mother of the Austens' neighbor Mrs. Lloyd, but if this is so, Jane Austen has taken the character of the bad mother and given her intelligence and energy.

It's true that Catherine Morland in *Northanger Abbey* experiences Bath society much as Jane Austen did, and almost loses her writing desk just as Jane Austen lost hers, probably during the period in which she was writing *Northanger Abbey*. But these explicitly matching autobiographical moments are rare.

We talk sometimes about "the world of Jane Austen," even though there is no such nicely furnished and easily identified world. Or, rather, there *is* a specific culture Austen inhabited, that century-lapping time frame 1775–1817, but it is a time too variable in its components and too poised for change for us to think of a seamless and stable "world." Much of what she puts down on the page is an England frozen in time, idealized, universalized.

Her novels are set in contemporary England, but her characters and their adventures are of the imagination—so much so that it might be thought to be a deliberate choice on her part to separate life and literature. She may, like many novelists who preceded and followed her, have been anxious to avoid injuring or embarrassing others by borrowing the material of their lives. The cruelty that colored her juvenilia had moderated, and she had become, if we can use her own word, more "particular."

Undoubtedly, like her contemporary novelists, she also saw novel making as an excursion to an invented world, rather than a meditation on her own. She mentions real places—London, Bath, Lyme Regis—but her heroines live in fictional villages—Highbury, Langbourn, Kellynch.

With great clarity, she marks off the territory she is willing or unwilling to tackle. Whole widths of human activity are excluded. The presence of the military, so crucial to a book like *Pride and Prejudice,* is sketched in, but the professional activities of soldiers, the historical context, is left out. There is no mention in the novels of new discoveries in science, though we know the Austens were familiar with Edward Jenner and his work with the cowpox vaccine. She reports faithfully the rhythms and concerns of daily discourse, but never strays into those conversations to which she could not have been a direct witness. We hear women talking to men, women talking to other women and to children, but we are not admitted to those closeted conversations when only men are present. In the same way, declarations of love between men and women are abstracted, summarized and indirectly delivered. As for sexual life, it is assumed rather than alluded to.

One of the widest areas of absence is the religious life, and this has led some to think that Jane Austen herself was an unbeliever. A daughter of the manse, a person who attended church with great regularity and took part in family prayers, Austen says not a word in her novels about the consolation of spiritual life. No one prays, no one blesses. No one is caught in the midst of worship. There is no evidence that she and Cassandra, in all the hours they spent together, discussed their faith or lack of it. It is true that the novels–and her life–are crowded with clergy. There is the good Dr. Shirley in *Persuasion,* the ridiculous Mr. Elton in *Emma,* the wise and witty Henry Tilney in *Northanger Abbey,* and always, of course, the presence of her own father, who unlike many lax churchmen of his day, lived among his parishioners as a Christian model. *Mansfield Park* examines, to some degree, the question of church ordination (at least this was Jane Austen's intention), but nowhere in the novels do we feel a surge of communion with the divine and certainly no trace of sentimental or platitudinous sermonizing. Her letters reflect, but only indirectly, a conventional belief in an afterlife, suggesting that she was able to accept the death of family and friends with some equanimity–but these are polite letters, letters of form. She did write a few prayers, all of them beautifully but conventionally composed and meant for the family's devotions:

Above all other blessings oh! God, for ourselves and our fellow-creatures, we implore thee to quicken our sense of thy mercy in the redemption of the world, of the value of that holy religion in which we have been brought up, that we may not, by our own neglect, throw away the salvation thou hast given us, nor be Christians only in name.

That exuberant "oh!" in the first line has Jane Austen's energy, and the reference to a "religion in which we have been brought up" hints at Jane Austen's spiritual obligation, but the rest of the prayer might have been written by any educated person of the time.

The exclusion of the religious impulse from her work may be no more than a belief that one's sacred life is a private matter, an attitude consistent with her times; the nineteenth-century evangelistic wave was just making itself known, and it was not a movement she felt comfortable with. Both piety and fervor would have embarrassed her, and others must have perceived this disinclination. Her cousin the Reverend Edward Cooper, who became an evangelical, wrote her cheerful and amusing letters—"He dares not write otherwise to me," she said, and the reader can almost imagine her chin going up and her eyebrows raised.

Still, it seems curious that she, a daughter and sister of clergymen, should not have touched more closely on the force, or at least the presence, of the spiritual in everyday life. Her brother Henry, shortly after her death, described her as being "thoroughly religious and devout," but her letters and novels present a more secular being.

Nor did she use much of the extraordinary dramatic material that was immediately available to her. Tact, and tenderness for her sister, may have kept her from creating a fiancé who dies of yellow fever shortly before his wedding. Nowhere in her novels is there a clergyman (like her father) who also keeps a school, one of whose pupils, Lord Lymington, exhibited dramatically disordered psychological symptoms. Nor is there any sideways reference to the extraordinary adventures of her cousin Eliza and Eliza's mother, Philadelphia.

It is a cliché to think of Jane Austen's life as being without event, since insanity, treason, illegitimacy, and elopement invaded her quiet family circle, and even, once or twice, criminal proceedings. In 1799 her aunt, Jane Leigh-Perrot, was accused of stealing a piece of lace from a Bath shop. For this presumed crime she was imprisoned for several weeks and tried at Taunton assizes, where she was eventually acquitted. The case was widely reported in the press, and it is impossible that Jane Austen would not have followed the developments day by day. Mrs. Austen, in fact, offered to send her two daughters to the county jail at Ilchester to keep company with their aunt, an offer that was refused—almost certainly to the relief of the Austen sisters.

To many novelists, this episode, with its class confrontation and its soaring sense of injustice and cruelty, would have presented the basis for powerful fiction. Not a mention of it appears in Jane Austen's fiction. Either it was unacceptable for her to drag in and further enlarge family difficulties or else she had other narratives she preferred to press forward. "She drew from nature; but whatever may have been surmised to the contrary, never from individuals," said her brother Henry in his Biographical Notice, which prefaced *Northanger Abbey* and *Persuasion* in 1818.

Ralph Waldo Emerson remained puzzled by Jane Austen's

novels, unable to grasp their value, complaining that they were, in the end, about nothing more than the making of marriages. Her attachment to her subject matter, as book after book rolled under her pen, may puzzle contemporary readers too, though we read her presumed narrowness in the question of subject matter differently today, seeing the *idea* of marriage in an enlarged metaphorical sense: a homecoming, a bold glance at the wider world of connection and commitment. Emerson may have been troubled by her claim to be a witness to what he saw as a minor narrative arc, since Jane Austen herself never married and perhaps was never entirely swept up into the full sweetness of courtship. But Austen's life and fiction rode different rails. *Pride and Prejudice,* that happiest of novels, erupted from a period of sadness, of personal disappointment. Elizabeth Bennet, a creation of Jane Austen's pen, achieved what Austen must have craved in her own life, particularly at the end of the eighteenth century when personal sadness clouded her consciousness, taking from her grasp liberation, love, wealth, happiness, resolution, and—most especially—a sense of control over her own existence.

9

THE FINAL YEARS at Steventon were the waiting years, the in-between years. Mrs. Austen suffered periodic illness, which required attendance. Her daughter Jane had the "dignity," as she put it rather caustically, of administering laudanum to her. Jane and Cassandra Austen, by now the ever available spinster sisters, were often called upon to give assistance in the homes of their relations; they alternated their visits to Godmersham, although it seems that Cassandra, who had by this time refined and perfected the role of aunt—and whose intelligence was less challenging to Edward's wife—was the preferred visitor. The periods of enforced separation yielded an exchange of letters between the two sisters that comments on their ongoing life and offers material for speculation on the nature of their relationship. The text of these letters spills with extravagant compliments, interrupted by little scolds and reproofs. "I expected to have heard from you this morning, but no letter is come," one of the scolds goes, from Jane to Cassandra. What was the tone of such recriminations? Was it the vagaries of the post that caused the consternation or Cassandra's inability to match her sister's letter-writing zeal?

When Jane Austen wrote to inform her sister of the birth of their brother James's new son, Cassandra returned her good wishes directly to James and his second wife, Mary. Jane Austen, who had provided the news in the first place, was not thanked, and she was not pleased at being overlooked. She wrote to Cassandra in a jocular but petulant voice: "I shall not take the trouble of announcing to you any more of Mary's Children, if, instead of thanking me for the intelligence, you always sit down and write to James." And then she added: "I am sure nobody can desire your letters as I do, and I don't think anyone deserves them so well." This same letter contains a poisonously chilly remark about a neighbor, which is perhaps inserted in a humorous effort to lift the cloud of blame that preceded it: "Mrs. Hall of Sherbourne was brought to bed yesterday of a dead child, some weeks before she expected, owing to a fright—I suppose she happened unawares to look at her husband."

We don't know what Cassandra made of such comments, and perhaps she made nothing—the reference may tap into an old joke of theirs and nothing more. Nor do we know how she received Jane Austen's remarks about her sister-in-law Mary following childbirth. Mary was indelicate, Jane reported crossly. She was untidy in her arrangements. She "does not manage things in such a way as to make me want to lay in myself."

Such remarks are telling, contributing to a sense of uneasiness between the sisters and to the suggestion, often raised, that Jane Austen avoided marriage because of the imposition and indignity of childbirth--and the very real danger of death. Certainly she was surrounded by terrifying examples; even her brother Edward's wife, Elizabeth, died eventually in the lottery of childbirth.

And yet, Jane Austen had not given up the hope that she might meet a husband, and she continued to attend local balls and parties. But when she reported to Cassandra in 1799 that "There was the same kind of supper as last Year & the same want of chairs," the drag of repetition and of failure is fully felt. And when we read in the same letter that "There was one Gentleman, an officer of the Cheshire, a very good looking young Man, who I was told wanted very much to be introduced to me;--but he did not want it quite enough to take much trouble in effecting it," we comprehend the undertow of discouragement and a reluctant acquiescence that doesn't quite manage to disguise itself.

In 1798 she spent time in Bath with her uncle Leigh-Perrot and his wife, and it was probably after this adventure that she settled down to a new work of fiction, an early version of *Northanger Abbey,* with the provisional title of *Susan,* the most explicitly literary of her novels. It is a narrative about a young girl's growing up, about living with authenticity, but it is also a novel-maker's comment on the art of the novel, as seen through the lens of the popular Gothic romances of her time.

Jane Austen's letters are filled with gossip, with visits, with shopping. Only occasionally does she talk about the act of writing itself, as in her well-known remark about how she worked on her small pieces of ivory or how she required only a few families to create the canvas for a novel. She wrote no essays about the novel form, and probably she read none. The novel was, during her lifetime, still in its infancy; its constructs, its subject matter, its self-consciousness were still being worked out. She read widely–good novels and rubbish–and evolved, slowly, her own notions of how the fictional world might reflect and interrogate the real world. In *Northanger Abbey* she mocks the silly Gothic novel and also the readers of such novels. She manages this with very little overt didacticism, allowing Catherine Morland to instruct us by her example while this young woman, the youngest of Austen's heroines, grows toward a new self-understanding in which the imagination is tempered by reason. From having no place of her own–she is one of ten children and not particularly beautiful or intelligent–she finds where she belongs through the exercise of her own powers, particularly the power of love. Loving Henry makes Henry notice Catherine and eventually love her.

Catherine Morland is lively and impressionable, and she has read enough Gothic romances to distort her vision of the world. *Northanger Abbey* mixes genres; it is a burlesque of the Gothic, just slightly reminiscent of Jane Austen's girlhood writing, and it is also the story of a young woman's education. The witty and attractive Henry Tilney, with whom Catherine falls in love, is one of Austen's most engaging creations. Like Darcy, he has the humanity to fall in love with a woman (girl?) who is inferior to him socially. He possesses the qualities of irony and integrity, and though he is a clergyman, he is utterly innocent of piety. *Northanger Abbey* is perhaps the only Jane Austen novel in which the heroine is in danger of being eclipsed by the hero. His sophistication counters Catherine's lack of worldliness, questions her absence of self-consciousness, and he loves her, tentatively at first, then endearingly, for what she has not yet become–and may never fully become.

Northanger Abbey is satire; epigrams lie everywhere on its surface: "A woman especially, if she have the misfortune of knowing any thing, should conceal it as well as she can." The tone here is arch and literary, as it is in the many personal asides and authorly intrusions, but we can see and hear the irony of the author's voice, an author who means exactly the opposite of what she is saying.

And yet, surprisingly, we can sometimes hear what sounds very much like a cry from the heart of the author herself. Describing Catherine, she says, "She had reached the age of seventeen, without having seen one amiable youth who could call forth her sensibility; without having inspired one real passion, and without having excited even any admiration, but what was very moderate and very transient." Catherine finds her man in the person of Henry Tilney, the first man she dances with at Bath, but not before experiencing the poignant sense of aloneness that Jane Austen must have known. This revelation of loneliness is all the more surprising since it appears in the novel that, of all Austen's work, most feels written as an entertainment.

The novel totters between this painful introspection and exclamations of assurance. Austen delivers, in chapter 5 of *Northanger Abbey*, a bold, spirited defense of the novel as a form, stepping off the page with a rare first person singular "I," cutting away from the frame of the novel for a moment and mocking those who say pretentiously, "I am no novel reader—I seldom look into novels." In novels, the narrator argues, "the greatest powers of the mind are displayed, in which, the most thorough knowledge of human nature, the happiest delineation of its varieties, the liveliest effusions of wit and humour are conveyed to the world in the best chosen language." Extraordinarily, this manifesto was delivered by a woman in her early twenties, whose own works had yet to be published—and wouldn't be for another dozen years.

The history of the *Northanger Abbey* manuscript is heartbreaking. It was completed in 1799 and read (and discussed and debated and weighed) by the Austen circle. Then it was put away for some years. In 1803, Jane Austen took it out from whatever drawer or closet it had been secreted in and revised it. What might the intervening years have added to the original idea of a young, impressionable girl confronting her future and facing the real world she was about to enter? It is commonly believed that Jane Austen's 1803 revisions were lighter and less extensive than those she imposed on her other novels. Still carrying the title *Susan*, the novel was sold to the London publisher Crosby for ten pounds. Austen must have been elated; she was twenty-eight years old, and this was her third mature novel—with *Sense and Sensibility* and

Pride and Prejudice still unpublished. At last she would find an audience.

In fact, the publisher did not bring out the novel as promised. Several years passed, and Jane Austen was never to know why a publisher would pay for a manuscript, advertise it, and then postpone its publication. Possibly the idea of the Gothic had lost its popularity, making a burlesque of the form somewhat absurd. Crosby may have lost confidence in a book that, in fact, is somewhat unsteady in its structure and certainty unorthodox. It has to be said that its elements—a young girl's struggle for love and happiness and a commentary on a fashionable literary strand, the Gothic—are not particularly well integrated. In 1809 the publisher offered her back her manuscript for the same ten pounds she had been paid, but she was unwilling or unable to take up the offer. Finally, in 1816, after the success of *Emma,* she did buy it back, revising it lightly and writing an "Advertisement" which describes the original publisher's delay and begs the patience of the reader, who might find a number of out-of-date allusions. It was finally published along with *Persuasion* in 1818, a year after Jane Austen's death, in a four-volume offering "By the Author of 'Pride and Prejudice,' 'Mansfield-Park,' &c."

An unsigned "Biographical Notice of the Author" prefaced the text, a brief sketch written, in fact, by Henry Austen, Jane's devoted brother. Jane Austen was, at last, introduced to the world. Henry is lavish in his praise of her person, her skill with music, drawing, and dancing, her devout Christianity, her taste and tact. He mentions Jane's debt to their father and how unsurprising it is that, considering her parentage, she "should, at a very early age, have become sensible to the charms of style, and enthusiastic in the cultivation of her own language. . . . Faultless herself, as nearly as human nature can be, she always sought, in the faults of others, something to excuse, to forgive or forget."

In this hymn of praise we can hear the voice of an adoring and grieving brother. But he was wrong when he claimed that everything flowed finished from his sister's pen; she was a fervent reviser of her own work, willing—as with *Sense and Sensibility*—to alter her basic novelistic structures. She happily rejiggered her point of view and, in the case of *Persuasion,* her ending.

And in one of his judgments brother Henry was far too moderate. Jane Austen's works, he prophesied, would eventually be "placed on the same shelf as the works of a D'Arblay and an Edgeworth." How far from the mark he was. Not only would she outdistance those all-but-forgotten names, but she would also find herself comfortably on the same shelf and in the good and steady company of Chaucer and Shakespeare.

10

THE NEXT NINE YEARS of Jane Austen's life were unsettled and, to those who interest themselves in her creative arc, almost entirely silent. This long silence, in the middle of a relatively short life, is bewildering. It is a silence that drives a wedge between her first three major novels and her final three: *Mansfield Park, Emma,* and *Persuasion.* The silence asks questions about the flow of Jane Austen's creative energies and about her reconciliation to the life she had been handed. She lived in a day when to be married was the only form of independence—and even then it was very much a restricted liberty. A married woman could achieve a home of her own, and with it a limited sphere of sovereignty. Why would Charlotte Lucas of *Pride and Prejudice* marry such a fool as Mr. Collins, who had already been turned down by Elizabeth Bennet? Because, in her late twenties, this was Charlotte's last—perhaps only—chance to escape the dominion of her parents and establish her own home. A home of one's own— we find this phrase, or a parallel expression, everywhere in Austen's work. Unlike Elizabeth Bennet, Charlotte Lucas would have suppressed her physical antipathy for conjugal life with Mr. Collins and, once assured of an heir and a spare, be able to construct a relatively separate existence–a marriage of compromise, of good sense and practicality.

What other possibilities were there? Within Jane Austen's immediate view there were no women artists, writers, or performers. Women of intellectual accomplishment were rare. What, besides marriage, might intervene? Her neighbor Mrs. Lefroy was intelligent and well read, but she was a wife and the mistress of a household. The witty, accomplished cousin Eliza provided, briefly, an example of an independent woman of unorthodox opinions, but even Eliza rather quickly formed a second marriage and surrendered her notions of independence.

Between the ages of twenty-five and thirty-three, the rhythms of Jane Austen's life–and the rhythms of her writing, too–were profoundly disturbed. She had been born in rural Steventon, and in her midtwenties was living there still, under the family roof, within the confines of her father's income and will. Early schooling and occasional travels–London, Kent, Bath–had taken her away from home for short periods, but home was what she loved best, home in its real sense–those comfortable and familiar Steventon surroundings. Home also meant psychological security–daily routines, old friends, acceptance, usefulness to those she loved, and the series of small accomplishments that gave purpose to her existence. Her sense of irony often throws biographers off course when assessing the Austen personality, but of two or three things we can be sure: She loved the natural world and drew strength from it. She thrived in circumstances that were steady and assured. Her creativity, her ability to put pen to paper, flowed from the reality of the familiar, the predictable.

Her attachment to nature and to the calm of Hampshire was genuine, and each temporary uprooting had brought, at its conclusion, renewal and the recaptured appreciation of the deep value she placed on home, the one place where she had a measure of autonomy and encouragement and where she felt at ease with her creative self.

In the year 1800 an enormous upheaval occurred in Jane Austen's settled life. The story is muddled and riddled with inconsistencies, probably because the most complete account of it was written many years after the actual event—almost seventy years, in fact, by Austen's niece Caroline. "My aunts had been away [from Steventon] a little while, and were met in the hall on their return [in fact, only Jane was present] by their mother who told them it was all settled, and they were going to live in Bath. My mother who was present said my aunt [Jane] was greatly distressed." There is no mention of fainting in this account, but the traditional tale is that Jane Austen fainted on hearing the news that the family was to leave its beloved Steventon and move to a place that was different in tone, feeling, and familiarity.

Can she really have fainted, she who in her earliest work mocked extravagant emotional responses, especially those assigned to women? The story accords well with her recently finished novel, *Susan*, but it is not securely embedded in eyewitness reports. She would have been shocked; there can be no doubt of that. The move to Bath came as a surprise to all the Austen family, though it is hard to believe that the possibility of such a move had not been previously discussed and debated. What were the old folks to do with themselves in their later years?

Every family has to deal with such questions. George Austen was seventy, a rather remarkable age to achieve in such a time; his wife was in up-and-down health, but her ups declared her to be still a woman of force and a full partner in a marriage that had always been an authentic partnership. The two of them lived in an isolated rural neighborhood. Their children had scattered, and even the two spinster daughters who lived at home were away at the time the parents concocted the Bath plan. What might this empty-house period of childlessness have given them? Possibly each was directed toward an honesty of approach; perhaps each of them spoke clearly. But could they have dismissed their daughters' wishes at that moment? There must have been ample time over the years for parents and children—the mother and father and their daughters—to sit around a breakfast table and discuss the future. What might they do in their old age to alleviate and alter their current arrangements, which could not possibly go on in the old, comfortable, and familiar way? Two spinster daughters still lived at home— the perplexing daughter Cassandra, who had survived, but barely, the death of her beloved fiancé, and Jane, the literary daughter, the writer of novels, the ironic, spiky daughter who was sometimes misunderstood.

The family, the scattered sons and the daughters, must have made their feelings known about the obvious possibilities in letters or in the rare opportunities when they came together. Steventon was their home; they were all attached to what Steventon meant, its compacted memories and embodiment of family happiness. At the same time, they must all have looked forward in time and wondered what sort of decision their parents would make. Negotiations would have been delicate; age carried power in families, particularly when the elderly were, like the senior Austens, in full possession of their senses. What the elders decided must be respected. Children, especially dependent children, had little choice but to go along with their parents' choices.

Nevertheless, for Jane Austen to leave a settled and comfortable rectory—its bucolic peace, its long family history—would have required extraordinary feats of adjustment.

Swallowing hard, she seems to have made that adjustment. It wasn't long before she was writing to Cassandra, "We have lived long enough in this neighbourhood, the Basingstoke balls are certainly on the decline, there is something interesting in the bustle of going away & the prospect of spending future summers by the sea or in Wales is very delightful."

These comments come soon after the first shock of the news, but they cannot be dismissed as mere bravery (the holidays by the sea and in Wales are meant to signal compensatory elements in a questionable new undertaking). She must have suspected, and resented, that her out-of-date country parents considered Bath to be good husband-hunting territory. The move to Bath might be seen as a desperate move, and even a sacrifice on the parents' part, to assist their daughters in achieving independence.

Jane Austen chatters on to her sister about accommodations to be had at Bath, about which furniture can or cannot be transported, and, rather endearingly, about her parents' bed that, it is decided, cannot be replaced and so must be removed to the new household. Her father's five hundred books must be sold or otherwise disposed of. Certain new arrangements concerning servants were to be made—and the particulars teasingly concealed from Mr. Austen, who, like Mr. Bennet in *Pride and Prejudice,* might offer objections. Austen is fanciful about these servants, the novelist already in top gear, laying out the scene: "We plan having a steady Cook & a young giddy Housemaid, with a sedate, middle aged Man, who is to undertake the double office of Husband to the former & sweetheart to the latter.—No Children of course to be allowed on either side." The pictures and much of the furniture were to go to her brother James and his wife Mary, an arrangement Jane clearly resented. James, the oldest of the Austen children, had always been the least favorite of her brothers, though he matches her in her attachment to home. He had gone away to Oxford as a young boy, but in a sense he had never left home, returning frequently and taking up parish duties close by, and now moving into Steventon and into his father's ecclesiastical position.

Jane Austen's tone in her letters to Cassandra is merry,

and expectant, and feverishly false. There is too much heartiness, and there are too many intervening letters after the first announcement that appear to have been destroyed by Cassandra. If we take Jane at her word, a new series of opportunities is opening up. If she had suffered a severe shock on hearing the news, she made at least the appearance of a rapid recovery and a quick recounting. Perhaps she remembered what her own Henry Tilney said in *Northanger Abbey:* "One day in the country is exactly like another." Or else she looked ahead to hear Anne Elliot in *Persuasion* say, "We live at home, quiet, confined, and our feelings prey upon us."

In Bath, there would be a refuge from those ever-present, preying thoughts. There would be new people to meet, new social patterns offered, new circumstances in which to re-create herself, and at the very least, new distractions from her predicament: her spinsterhood, now established, and the lack of money to bring to any marriage bargain that might present itself. Bath was also a place from which excursions might be made, and there were the possibilities of visits from other family members. She must have weighed these conditions carefully, whatever her first reaction to her father's decision to move to Bath, though the question remains: Did other choices occur to her? Were other possibilities offered?

Decisions surrounding the move were almost immediately being made for her, and these she resisted. A new degree of petulance radiates from her correspondence. Her parents and sister suggested how she might dispose of some of her possessions. Politely, tartly, she refused. "You are very kind," she wrote to Cassandra, "in planning presents for me to make, & my Mother has shewn me exactly the same attention—but as I do not chuse to have Generosity dictated to me, I shall not resolve on giving my Cabinet to Anna [her niece] till the first thought of it has been my own."

Mrs. Austen, while acknowledging that her family comprised two unmarried daughters, was able to think of her life without them. In 1797 she welcomed a new daughter-in-law, Mary Lloyd, by saying, "I look forward to you as a real comfort to me in my old age, when Cassandra is gone into Shropshire & Jane—the Lord knows where." Cassandra, in this quote, possesses context; Jane remains unpredictable, a young woman whose ability to offer comfort and companionship to an aged parent is doubtful. There is a great shrug of resignation in such a casual dismissal, and there is also a suggestion of rupture between parent and child. The two daughters were troublesome, and the younger daughter in particular. Mr. and Mrs. Austen must hatch their plans without taking them into consideration.

11

IN CHAPTER TWO of *Northanger Abbey* there is a paragraph that begins exuberantly: "They arrived at Bath. Catherine was all eager delight." This exclamation launches the novel, bringing Catherine, in effect, from the country to the city, and from girlhood to what will follow.

Jane Austen, and Cassandra too, when informed that they were to move from Steventon, must have asked, why Bath? True, Bath was a golden city, and not just because of the color of the local building stone—Jane Austen, in fact, expressed complaint about the "glare" of the fresh stone facades. The city glowed with newness, with history, with harmonious architecture, with the positive and curative effects of its hot springs, with optimism and with gentility. Jane Austen was familiar with London from a few short visits and knew her parents would never settle there. Bath was the only other urban center she knew, and it was a logical retirement location, which she must have realized once she had absorbed the idea that her parents were really to leave Steventon behind—and how reasonable and even predictable that they should choose Bath over their other favorites, Lyme Regis and Sidmouth.

Bath in 1800 would have presented a happy compromise for them, since, with its approximately 34,000 inhabitants, it was decidedly urban but without the stress associated with London. Tradesmen had sprung up everywhere along its streets. Unlike other growing urban centers, this city catered to people who had come from elsewhere, bringing money with them and the desire for pleasure and relaxation.

And Bath was familiar to the Austens, being the previous site of happy holidays and family reunions. Mrs. Austen's brother, Leigh-Perrot, and his wife lived there in some luxury. The parents of Jane Austen had been married in 1764 at the old Walcot Church at the edge of the city. An entry in the Parish register reads: "Geo Austen Bachelor of the Parish of Steventon, County of Hampshire to Cassandra Leigh, Spinster. Married by license this 26 April . . ." Here, too, is the recorded death notice of Mrs. Austen's father. And in 1805, just five years after his retirement, Mr. Austen himself was buried in the Walcot churchyard: "Under this stone rest the remains of the Rev. George Austen, Rector of Steventon . . ."

Bath is in Somerset, about a hundred miles from London. It existed because of its natural hot springs and their healing properties, which were known to the Romans, who built a city on the site. The elaborate baths, and a temple dedicated to the goddess Minerva, had long since fallen into decay and forgetfulness, and were not excavated until 1871. Astonishingly, the Austen family would have known nothing about ancient Bath, though it is hard to believe there were not legends in circulation and perhaps even the odd artifact. In the sixteenth century Queen Elizabeth I granted the city a charter, and with this stroke made it a fashionable pleasure resort. (Today Margaret Thatcher comes here to relax; the Clintons have dropped in and so have a number of film stars, including Elizabeth Taylor and Demi Moore. There can be no doubt that name-dropping was, and continues to be, part of fabled Bath.)

Art and history conspired to bless the city, as did the great spurt of economic growth in the late seventeenth century. Roads had improved—the London-Bath road was the best-maintained artery in England—making it easier for people to travel in search of improved health and also to advance themselves in society. As modern Bath emerged, it was as a planned city with an integrated architecture, unlike anything else in Britain. During the early years of the eighteenth century, streets were paved and well lit so that people could come and go in safety and could alight from their carriages without finding themselves ankle deep in mud (Jane Austen's novels are filled with references to this particular inconvenience). Commerce arrived in the form of elegant shops, circulating libraries, and banks.

But people needed accommodation for their short or extended stays, and so construction was soon underway to provide apartments for these many visitors. A theater was established in the middle of the eighteenth century, with well-known actors arriving from London and performing the latest plays. The baths themselves ensured that sociability flourished, and from them evolved the Assembly Rooms, where visitors gathered to drink the rather vile-tasting waters and to enjoy concerts. Dinners, dances, card parties, and chance encounters in the shopping streets brought drama to everyday life. It also brought a different sort of opportunity to the city, which became a place where marriages could be contracted and business could be done. Bath was, in short, an entrepreneurial dream.

It was a retreat for the wealthy, a spa, a place of sociability and fashion—all these things. But by 1800, when the Austens settled there, it was thirty or forty years out of date and more a destination for retired professionals like George Austen than for those in search of pleasure. Newer resorts and spas, like Brighton and Cheltenham, were attracting the young and adventurous.

Did Jane Austen's parents, in choosing Bath, believe that the city might be an opportunity to exhibit, and perhaps find husbands for, their two daughters? It may have been one of many considerations; it may also be that they didn't fully appreciate the fact that Bath was no longer as fashionable as it had once been. Or they might even have considered its old-fashioned flavor an advantage, a form of protection and unconscious consolation for Cassandra and Jane, whose futures as spinsters now seemed almost certain.

Bath became the main setting for two of Jane Austen's novels, *Northanger Abbey* and, later, *Persuasion,* and in these two background glimpses of the city we can see the social forces moving from the dynamic in the earlier novel to the staid in *Persuasion,* where both compromise and reconciliation colored what Bath society had to offer. Each of the other novels, even the slight *Lady Susan,* touches tangentially on Bath. Wickham, in *Pride and Prejudice,* escapes to Bath in his later life, leaving marital dullness behind. And where else should Mr. Elton of *Emma* go to seek a wife, especially a foolish wife, but to Bath? Other characters are called to Bath on business, or they travel there for reasons of health or to take refuge in times of trouble. Bath, real or mythical, was part of Jane Austen's geography, a place and also an idea. It had lost some of its excitement and edge in the late eighteenth century, but never its respectability or its healing powers. Jane Austen's use of Bath demonstrates her precise understanding of new attitudes toward money and leisure. With the accurate placement of Bath in her contemporary universe she proves herself an astute reporter on sociological change.

12

TOWARD THE END of the old century, the Austen family—the parents and two daughters—embarked on the matter of moving house. This took time and patience. It also took careful economic management. Fragile furniture was cheaper to replace than to move, so it was finally decided that only the family beds could be taken to the new home in Bath. A favorite sideboard was abandoned, and the Pembroke tables. Not surprisingly, old painted sets from the family theatricals in the barn were left behind, and with them the childhood memories of a full, vibrant family life. Jane Austen's pianoforte was another of the losses of the move, the pianoforte on which she played every morning not for an audience, but for her own enjoyment. George Austen's five-hundred-book library went up for sale, and realized a disappointing sum, though many of the volumes devolved to his son James. Books, music, mementos, familiar furniture, the beauty of a mature garden—all this was to be surrendered. Perhaps even worse was the parting with old friends like Martha Lloyd, Anne Lefroy, and the Bigg-Withers at Manydown Park.

Family feelings went sour during the relocation, at least between Jane Austen and her brother James, who, with his wife Mary, was to move into the rectory. Those items that were not sold or otherwise disposed of went directly to James's family, and Jane's letters of the time give the impression that she and Cassandra and her parents were being insensitively pushed from the family home, or at least politely hurried along and encouraged in their move to Bath.

Austen was obliged to leave the countryside she loved and become a city dweller. Even before departing from Steventon, she was, like Anne Elliot in *Persuasion,* "dreading the possible heats of September in all the white glare of Bath, and grieving to forego all the influence so sweet and so sad of the autumnal months in the country . . ." The countryside, especially a landscape as familiar as Jane Austen's corner of Hampshire, fostered contemplation, and was not only unthreatening but also heartening. She was rooted in its midst. We don't often hear from her the trilling tones of the exuberant nature lover, but we can read in all the novels, and in all the major characters, an acceptance—and a preference—for country life. Would Mr. Knightley, that inveterate reader of agricultural reports, pull up stakes and take Emma off to live in London? Or in Bath? Never. It would be unthinkable.

There can be little question that Jane Austen's rather fragile frame of creativity was disturbed following the move to Bath. Since returning from school at the age of eleven, she had found her place in her family, amusing those around her with her writing, winning their approval, and then growing to maturity and learning to divert herself with her carefully crafted novels, novels in which young women–Elizabeth, Catherine, Elinor and Marianne–find ways to liberate themselves from their circumstances. Her own existence as the younger daughter in a large family had reached a point of stasis, but her creative life soared within her particular set of circumstances, in which she was protected, encouraged, and–it must be said–left largely alone. She had, after two or perhaps three enforced separations, to a foster home during infancy and then to school, mastered the delicate trick of living within her family and, through her imaginative work, leaving them behind. Readers are sure to be puzzled by Jane Austen's silence in the ensuing years unless they understand how unarmored she was against change, against a new and superficial society, against those who had not known her from childhood and who were unfamiliar with her history and the direction of her thoughts. Bath was a showcase city; everyone, and everything, was up for display. Display was why people went to Bath: to see and be seen, to judge and be judged.

Austen had also witnessed the phenomenon faced by the younger children of large families who watch their older brothers and sisters drift off into the world, leaving them behind in a diminished family nest, often with aging parents who are unwilling or unable to renegotiate the parental role and who are more and more focused on the remaining "children." This not-at-all-uncommon situation requires immense tolerance on all sides and subtle readjustments that call for an openness of expression. It is difficult to imagine such a psychological rearrangement taking place at Steventon, and even harder to envision a free exchange of ideas. The uneasiness of the situation might be recognized on all sides, but be too awkward to be brought to the surface. In Jane Austen's novels daughters grow up and very often become their parents' advisers. In her own family it seems this did not happen; her parents continued to act, as they had always done, without her counsel in decisions that radically affected her life.

Jane Austen was particularly adrift at the time her parents announced the move to Bath. Cassandra, her only real confidante, was, during those months, visiting in Kent where the shock of impending change must have been muffled by distance and by distraction. Jane's letters to her in 1800 and the first part of 1801 are particularly sour. We can read her loss and confusion through the satiric bite of her observations, and there is, as well, a sad sense of lowered consequence. She ordered two brown dresses in January of 1801, one for herself and one for her mother, and insisted that the shades of brown must vary slightly so that the difference between them would provide a topic of conversation. There was much going on in the world at the time, including the immensely popular heroics of Admiral Nelson and the naval successes of Austen's own brother Captain Frank Austen, but Jane Austen, twenty-five years old, felt herself reduced to discussing shades of brown and sniping at neighbors: "Mr Dyson as usual looked wild, & Mrs. Dyson as usual looked big." There is in the letters of this period very little of the buoyancy that had formerly compensated for her verbal thrusts, no little darts of joy or the hope of intervening circumstances. She was a spinster daughter, living with elderly parents, exchanging her family home for rented rooms in a city where she would have no real intellectual companions other than her sister, Cassandra. Her self-mockery stops well short of humor.

She never announced herself to be in a state of depression, but certainly she understood the condition. Both Fanny Price and Marianne Dashwood (*Mansfield Park* and *Sense and Sensibility*) are immobilized by sadness and powerlessness, and even Emma is paralyzed, momentarily, when brought face to face with her own imperfections. Jane Austen was too private and too wary of self-pity to declare her state. We apprehend it, today, through the bitterness of her correspondence, but mostly through the abrupt cessation of her novels, a flow of words that had poured from her pen since late childhood. Now it dried up. As a writer she was disabled and profoundly discouraged.

It would be almost ten years, when she was approaching her thirty-fifth birthday, before she returned to the productive working habits of her young womanhood. It is impossible to say whether she suffered from depression or distraction. She had been dislocated in both time and space, taken abruptly to a new and fashionable world, and it was not one she would have chosen.

It might be thought that a move would stimulate a young writer. Her nephew James Edward Austen-Leigh, setting down the Austen memoir years later, seems to have been no more than mildly perplexed by his aunt's midlife silence, saying only that it "might rather have been expected that fresh scenes and new acquaintance would have called forth her powers." Virginia Woolf has written insightfully on this very topic. A writer, she maintains, does not need stimulation, but the opposite of stimulation. A writer needs regularity, the same books around her, the same walls. A writer needs self-ordered patterns of time, her own desk, and day after profitable day in order to do her best work.

Jane Austen and her family moved house several times during their Bath years, and from what we know these rooms grew progressively smaller and less comfortable. She also suffered a number of deaths during the period: the gradual collapse and death of her cousin Eliza's fifteen-year-old son; the accidental death of her great friend Mrs. Lefroy; and, above all, the demise of her father in 1805. Austen has a reputation for being philosophical about death and for dry detachment and acceptance of its reality. The letter she writes to her brother Francis informing him of their father's death seems exceptionally cool, and a reader of Jane Austen is soon aware of how seldom tragic death intrudes on the pages of her fiction. But death, and particularly the death of her father, must have affected her deeply. He had fostered her talent, providing her with a careful critical eye and with the more practical gifts of writing paper and a writing desk.

His death also placed his wife and daughters in a precarious economic state. There were no pensions for the widows and children of clergymen. Mrs. Austen and Cassandra were each left with a small income, but Jane Austen had nothing. Early on she must have perceived the way in which reality rebukes fiction since her heroines, with their intelligence and vigor, are always able to grasp some means of self-preservation while she, their creator, is left helpless—with no income and no choices.

Her brothers Frank, James, and Henry all offered what they could to the three women, which was not a great deal. But Edward, the wealthy owner of Godmersham, and of huge landholdings in Kent and Hampshire, seems to have taken a rather nonchalant part in providing for his mother and sisters. It was only years later that he wakened to their circumstances, pushed a button, and provided them with a permanent home at Chawton—where Jane Austen, once again, became a functioning writer.

13

THE CREATIVE SILENCE of Jane Austen's middle years gestures toward other silences. Of George, her handicapped brother placed in foster care when he was a child, there is not one word, though he lived into old age.

Of her mother's uncertain health and difficult disposition there are only covert suggestions. With the Reverend George Austen's death, the relationships in the little family must have shifted, the newly impoverished mother and two daughters rubbing up against each other in new, more immediate ways, and probably with greater distress.

What other events intrude on this long midlife silence? A sort of half story exists about Jane visiting a Devon resort and becoming friendly with a young man who showed an interest in continuing the friendship, and then died. This small chip of an incident, if it did occur, was related by Cassandra to her niece Caroline years later and is, sadly, unreliable in its turnings, being too much a mirror image of Cassandra's tragic engagement and too much the traditional material of opaque family legends, which represent, perhaps, the wish to sprinkle a little fairy dust on a life that was sadly lacking in romance.

Rumors and legends also attend a marriage proposal that Jane Austen received–and accepted–in early December of 1802. She and Cassandra were away from Bath, visiting at a large country house near Steventon. The Bigg-Wither family of Manydown Park were very old friends, and their two sons and seven daughters had intermingled freely with the Austen children as they grew to adulthood. Catherine and Alethea Bigg, in particular, were close to Cassandra and Jane, and possessed the same high spirits.

Harris Bigg-Wither, since the death of his older brother, was the heir to Manydown Park, a rather shy and shambling young man of twenty-one, with a serious stutter and an oddly blunted intelligence. To everyone's astonishment, he approached Jane Austen during her December visit and asked her to be his wife. She accepted, then almost immediately regretted her decision.

The age difference between them was only six years, not a serious point of consideration, though it is quite clear that she did not love him. The heroes of all her novels are bookish men–Henry Tilney, Darcy, Mr. Knightley–and Harris Bigg-Wither was an overgrown country schoolboy with very little inclination for learning. She did, to be sure, long to marry. She was just days away from her twenty-seventh birthday and facing the reality of what that might mean. Age twenty-seven had a meaningful ring to it. Marianne in *Sense and Sensibility* proclaims, "A woman of seven and twenty can never hope to feel or inspire affection again." Austen's own words written a few years earlier must have rattled in her head, and she would already have been unsettled by a surprise offer from an old family friend and one she had never thought of in a romantic light.

It is certain that being the mistress of the great estate of Manydown would have been a temptation to Jane Austen, growing older and living in rented rooms with her parents in Bath. Undoubtedly, she was fond of the boyish, awkward Harris, whom she had known all her life, but the intimacy of marriage was a different matter.

She had expressed her thoughts about marriage as a "compact of convenience," in which each partner benefits in some way. Charlotte Lucas, accepting the egregious Mr. Collins as a husband, explains: "I am not romantic you know. I never was. I ask only a comfortable home." Jane Austen also longed for a home; all her novels concern themselves with this longing. But the reality, when represented in the bumptious form of Harris Bigg-Wither himself, was untenable.

During the night following the proposal she resolved to break her agreement. Almost certainly she consulted Cassandra. The marriage would bind the two families even closer together and would give Jane a home of her own, but nothing could alter the person of Harris Bigg-Wither and the very probable revulsion she felt for him. Emma in *The Watsons* announces that she can think of nothing worse "than [to] marry a man I did not like." And years later, advising her niece Fanny, who was in the delicate position of having encouraged a young man in his hopes, Austen wrote, "Anything is to be preferred or endured rather than marrying without Affection."

She knew, too, and so did Cassandra, that marriage would permanently reshape their extraordinarily close sisterly relationship. In accepting the marriage proposal, she must have felt she had made a dutiful decision, one that would ease the worry and financial strain of the Austen family. But the role of martyr was too heavy to bear. The morning after the proposal she confronted her fiancé and informed him of her change of mind.

The situation was immensely uncomfortable on all sides. Jane and Cassandra left the house immediately and fled to Steventon, where they demanded that their brother James take them home to Bath the next day. They were in a state of great distress, insisting that they must leave the neighborhood at once. The scene is dramatic and unforgettable: the tableau of the trembling women who, during what must have been a sleepless night, came to a decision that might possibly rupture relations between two old families. Jane Austen was exposed as a woman who for once lacked good sense, first leaping into a serious agreement without adequate reflection, then embarrassing herself and the members of two households. Cassandra, fleeing with Jane and sharing her humiliation, can be seen as the persuasive force behind the change of plan. Her own concerns, her wish to protect or limit her sister's future, are caught up in the net of intrigue.

The story of the marriage proposal, its hasty acceptance

and its reversal twelve hours later, entered the leaves of the Austen legend. Each family member had a theory, an explanation, about why Jane, normally so determined in her resolutions, so *sensible,* should have entered into a hasty agreement and then, with great clumsiness, extricated herself. What a pity, some of them must have said. Her life would have been more comfortable, more rewarding, and there might even have been children. An averted catastrophe, others must have said; for Jane Austen was not Charlotte Lucas. She was not a woman who could marry without love and without even a measure of respect.

His heart intact, or so it would seem, Harris Bigg-Wither proceeded to marry Anne Howe Frith two years later and produce a family of ten children. Jane Austen, having survived this excruciating experience in 1802, returned to Bath and to a future in which her chances of marriage declined with each birthday. She must have meditated on her stupidity and grieved from time to time about a life she had rejected. In her letters she grows increasingly silent on the subject of balls and parties, and of the possibility that she might yet meet her ideal husband.

There was an injurious silence, too, from the London publisher Crosby about the publication of *Northanger Abbey,* or *Susan,* as it was then called, which had first been accepted—and its publication advertised—in 1803. The silence on the part of the publisher went on and on, year after year without explanation. Why didn't she contact them and demand an explanation? She must have been, like any beginning novelist, unsure of the power arrangements between author and publisher. Certainly she wasn't accustomed to dealing with publishers; publishers existed in another realm of life—in London, with their own habits and expectations, and their own majestic decisions.

She had already, with *First Impressions,* been cruelly cut down; now, at least, with the help of her brother Henry and his connections, she had obtained a promise of publication, and one she was disinclined to stir by annoying letters of inquiry. And undoubtedly she expected to hear at any moment that the novel was in print, that she was, at last, a published author, perhaps even a highly praised new voice. Meanwhile, it was difficult to invest her energies in a serious new work when not one of her finished novels had been launched in the world.

Novelists do not write into a void. They require an answering response, an audience of readers outside their family circle, and they also need the approval that professional publication brings. Next week, next year—surely she would hear soon. This hope must have remained with her, but the impulse to produce more novels withered.

A series of discouragements conspired against her in the middle of her life, and the resulting silence means that everything we know of her during this period is a guessing game, a question that leads around and around to an even greater silence.

14

THE LONG YEARS of silence had to be filled somehow. Jane Austen, restless and dissatisfied with life in Bath, busied herself with long hikes—she once described herself as "a desperate walker"—and with visits to Lyme Regis and other holiday resorts.

And in 1803 she began a new novel, *The Watsons*, which she never finished. We are left with about 17,000 words of promising dramatic action, perhaps one quarter of a finished novel, and then an abrupt halt in 1805, probably at the time of her father's death—just as she was about to dramatize the death of Mr. Watson in the novel and leave Emma Watson an orphan.

Jane Austen was not, on the whole, an autobiographical novelist, but this fragment, *The Watsons*, presses closer to her own life and predicament than any of her other works. The four Watson daughters are unmarried, and they are poor. Their father is a clergyman and in poor health. With his impending death, their situation is about to worsen rather than improve—unless, that is, they can find husbands. Emma Watson, who in her vivacity and intelligence resembles Elizabeth Bennet, has been raised not within the family, but by a more cultivated aunt, somewhat in the same manner as Edward Austen, who was plucked out of the respectable but struggling family at Steventon and adopted by wealthy relations.

Even closer to the autobiographical bone may be the question of intense sibling rivalry between the Watsons—treachery, in fact, between two of the sisters. The altercation is shocking, and there has been speculation that a degree of difficulty existed between Jane and Cassandra Austen, who have commonly been regarded as being devoted to each other. But signs are apparent, and not just in *The Watsons,* that there was some strain between them. In their later years they were frequently separated, alternating their visits to relations, and these arrangements may have been deliberately put in place by a family that recognized the situation.

Jane, the younger sister, the writer of great novels, always, superficially at least, deferred to Cassandra, so much so that some of her letters to her older sister have a suggestion of appeasement, the wish to amuse at any cost and the refusal to take herself seriously as a correspondent.

Sisterly relationships are presented with great warmth in the early novels, but they cool noticeably in *Mansfield Park,* where the Bertram sisters are on poor terms, and in *Persuasion,* where Anne ardently dislikes her silly, snobbish sisters and makes no apology for her feelings. As for Emma Woodhouse and her sister Isabella, they are widely separated by age and geography so that they scarcely seem sisters at all.

There is no hard evidence that Cassandra betrayed her sister in any way, although she must have played an advisory role in the broken engagement with Bigg-Wither, something that Jane Austen couldn't help adding to her stock of experience and that she may have carried forward, consciously or unconsciously, into the fabric of *The Watsons*.

As the novel opens, Emma has returned to her family and, like her sisters, is assumed to be in the serious business of husband hunting. Local society conspires with this drive, and the story takes off quickly in the direction of matchmaking. A number of available males are introduced, and Emma, again like Elizabeth, appoints herself the gentle judge of her suitors' various moral achievements and failures.

The writing is often charming, with an openness of expression that signals a new determination to describe the plight of women, particularly the fact that women of Jane Austen's class had nothing but marriage to rescue them from their parental home. A marriage of love was almost always out of reach in real life, though all of Jane Austen's heroines, before and following *The Watsons*, achieve just that. The reality was that women without money were forced into marriages of compromise, which was what Jane Austen herself had recently rejected when she withdrew her promise to Harris Bigg-Wither. A number of misgivings must have followed that decision, since the alternative was spinsterhood, with its various shames and confinements.

Jane Austen was a writer who kept her manuscripts close at hand and who tinkered with them endlessly. Other writers burn or shred their unfinished efforts, but she had enough regard for her tentative drafts to keep them safe. The fragmentary story of the Watsons has survived and come down to a contemporary readership that appreciates its energy and promise and, most particularly, the light it shines on Jane Austen's thoughts in the early years of the century while she was living in Bath with her parents, after having escaped marriage by a whisker.

She discussed the proposed trajectory of *The Watsons* with Cassandra, who passed on the novel's narrative structure much later in life. There was to be a happy ending, which would surprise no one. Emma Watson would reject the attentions of Lord Osborne, who would have brought security and comfort to the whole Watson family, and marry a man of simplicity and sincerity, capable of offering the gift of love. The makings of a fairy tale are here: the poor but noble-spirited young woman—Emma Watson—who refuses to cave in to an unjust social norm. To pursue a man in order to improve one's situation, she tells her sister Elizabeth, "is a sort of thing that shocks me; I cannot understand it. Poverty is a great Evil, but to a woman of Education & feeling it ought not be, it cannot be the greatest." Elizabeth, an older, more experienced sister, is less sanguine. For her there is little to look forward to.

Why did Jane Austen abandon the project? She had invented an attractive heroine and placed her in a promising moral and social dilemma. She had established a firm narrative arc, and there is very little to support the idea that she might have turned the tables on her readers, investing Lord Osborne with an unsuspected worth.

A dazzling episode occurs in the opening pages of the novel. Emma attends a neighborhood ball, and instead of the familiar scene of the girl without a partner, we see a young boy, abandoned and longing to dance. Emma acts forcefully by rescuing him from his lonely humiliation: "'I shall be very happy to dance with you sir, if you like it' said she, holding out her hand with the most unaffected good humour." She takes him as her dancing partner, spontaneously and joyfully, and with natural respect. She might have been thought silly or aggressive, but instead she is perceived by those at the ball to have acted with great tact and natural kindness.

There is not a great deal of love for children in Jane Austen's work, which is not surprising since she was often saddled with the care of her many nieces and nephews. But this scene from *The Watsons* draws on the early and more innocent response she had to the vulnerability of children—and to the pleasure of dancing.

The scene is a joyous set piece, a chance for the reader to know and appreciate Emma's rare qualities. Soon after, though, the story of Emma and her sisters hardens. The desperate struggle to marry becomes a bitter impasse. Elizabeth, Emma's older sister, puts it plainly: "You know we must marry—I could do very well single for my own part.—A little company, and a pleasant ball now and then, would be enough for me, if one could be young forever, but my father cannot provide for us, and it is very bad to grow old and be poor and laughed at."

This subject, the impossible bargaining position of single

women, becomes too quickly the only subject. The novel dwindles, narrows, and loses sparkle. The men are never brought fully to life. And perhaps this realization encouraged Austen to put the manuscript away.

The subject may have been too close to her own recent experience to permit the grace and humor and saving side stories of *Pride and Prejudice*. For a writer who had taken pains to avoid autobiography, the developments in the Watson family were becoming overly delicate to handle. And she must have been aware that she was covering the same territory as in her earlier novels, but with less buoyancy, bringing instead a harsh cry of rebellion and outrage.

Her nephew James Edward Austen-Leigh, known by his aunt as Edward, offered an interesting conjecture about Jane's failure to finish the novel. She might have placed the four Watson sisters at too low a level of society, he believed, and "like a singer who has begun on too low a note, she discontinued the strain." It is true that the Watsons are less fashionable and less financially secure than Austen's other families, but they are not nearly as low on the social index as Fanny Price's awful Portsmouth family in *Mansfield Park*; they are less desperate for respectability than the Bateses in *Emma*, less beleaguered than Mrs. Smith in *Persuasion*.

It is also true that Edward Austen-Leigh felt a custodial duty toward the Austen clan, wanting always to present the family in a respectable position. Low life frightened him, possibly, in a way that it did not frighten his aunt. Furthermore, the social balance in England had taken on immense freight between Jane Austen's death in 1817 and the publication of Edward Austen-Leigh's history at the height of the Victorian age, 1870. Nuances of *politesse* had multiplied. Certain social barometers had shifted. Ladies no longer helped with meals or with the washing of teacups. They had abandoned the spinning of fibers for the family linen. The wearing of pattens, crude, almost medieval shoes, was taken for granted by the practical Austen family, just the thing for muddy roads, but was seen by Jane Austen's nephew as a sign of vulgarity. His history of his aunt and her family is full of such tensions. There is so much he cannot understand or refuses to understand, and so much family material for which he would like to offer up apology. The document is endearing for just this confusion of perceptions and for the light it casts on a shift of morals and manners in nineteenth-century England. We cannot read it today as precise truth, but we can appreciate its desire to map the life of his celebrated aunt in the light of his own time. The intensity of personal detail is a gift. As a young man he attempted to write a novel, and the memoir does move forward with a pleasing novelistic pace. Many of his conjectures are imaginative. Others are gross reductions: "Of events her life was singularly barren; few changes and no great crisis ever broke the smooth current of its course."

Jane Austen is sometimes thought of as being confined by her extremely narrow social view, but her work reveals a far wider optic lens. The Watson family was old-fashioned; they were frugal; they were necessarily engaged in the ongoing domestic labor of their home, their laundry, their small economies.

It is telling that *The Watsons* is the only major work by Austen that was written in Bath, that alien territory. Her early work was composed at her girlhood home in Steventon, and the later novels–*Mansfield Park, Emma,* and *Persuasion*–in the settled tranquillity of Chawton. This single effort was brought to life–or at any rate to a stillbirth–in a city that she found uncongenial and at a time in her life when her self-confidence was at its lowest ebb.

15

THE ABILITY to sustain long works of fiction is at least partially dependent on establishing a delicate balance between solitude and interaction. Too much human noise during the writing of a novel distracts from the cleanliness of its overarching plan. Too little social interruption, on the other hand, distorts a writer's sense of reality and allows feeling to "prey" on the consciousness—to place Jane Austen's (or Anne Elliot's) own words in a slightly different context.

For every writer the degree of required social involvement or distance must be differently gauged, but novelists who take refuge in isolated log cabins tend to be a romantic minority, or perhaps even a myth. Most novelists, knowing that ongoing work is fed by ongoing life, prize their telephones, their correspondence, and their daily rubbing up against family and friends.

Jane Austen, who wrote intensely social novels, was an intensely social being. "We did not walk long in the Crescent yesterday," she wrote Cassandra; "it was hot and not crouded [sic] enough." Moments of solitary meditation are relatively rare in her work. Changes of mood or intention are most often framed within conversations—during supper parties, while taking long walks, or mending linen in the sitting room. Two, three, four people are present; their participation is the mechanism that moves the action forward. Whatever is proposed or considered finds a response, either a concert of agreement or a choir of dissonance. There may be a knock on the door at any moment or a carriage passing on the roadway, and these developments must be registered. Individual actions have social consequences in Jane Austen's fiction, and the same can be assumed for her life. She admired—as Mr. Knightley in *Emma* admired—an open temper, but recognized that what was deeply private was likely to remain unspoken and unwritten, except in the form of gesture; and for this she possessed an unequivocal skill. Her novels can be read through their moments of confrontation and also through the light that glances and gathers around the many silences.

For most of her life Jane Austen had little opportunity to indulge in solitude. She herself was almost never beyond the reach of family, or out of touch with friends. An empty room in the early years at Steventon would have been a rarity; the various small rented quarters in Bath must also have prohibited the privacy a writer cherishes. Later, life at Chawton presented similar problems: four women (for Martha Lloyd had joined the family by then) inhabiting a few crowded rooms, together with the comings and goings of servants and the arrival, most often unannounced, of visitors.

To write is to be self-conscious, as Jane Austen certainly knew. What flows onto paper is more daring or more covert than a writer's own voice, or more exaggerated or effaced. This gap between consciousness and text is always ready to freeze the movement of the pen, particularly when the act of writing is done in the presence of others. Austen had no study of her own, no cozy refuge arranged for her quiet convenience. The encouragement of her imagination did not arise from conditions offered her by others. Composing–and this is the term she generally used–was done in the family sitting room, and it is said, famously, that she quickly covered over the manuscript page when someone else entered unexpectedly, or slipped the pages inside her small mahogany desk.

As a woman of her class, it was expected that she would be accompanied on outings. Leaving her childhood friends behind, she managed to find new companions at Bath who were willing to share her long walks. They may not always have been agreeable company, but they were convenient for her purpose. Her travels in England–and she never visited more than a handful of counties–were undertaken with a family member by her side: her mother, her sister, one of her many brothers, or else a trusted family servant.

She may have chafed at her lack of solitude, but a life of social engagement was what she knew and what in the end nourished her fiction. Friendship was one of the values of the eighteenth century into which she was born. It was sometimes spoken of as though it were a new invention. Her own family depended on their neighbors' warm hospitality, and many of these friendships endured throughout her life.

There is even a sense that she was able to extract more pleasure from her social encounters than others did and that she prided herself on that ability. A last-minute invitation to dine at Ashe Park was immediately accepted. "We had a very quiet evening," she wrote Cassandra. "I believe Mary [her sister-in-law] found it dull, but I thought it very pleasant. To sit in idleness over a good fire in a well-proportioned room is a luxurious sensation.–Sometimes we talked & sometimes we were silent; I said two or three amusing things, & Mr. Holder made a few infamous puns." It is clear that on this occasion she experienced several overlapping sensations: that there is human comfort in such evenings and also the possibility for drama, even if it were not in the end fulfilled; that her own appreciation of such moments outdistanced Mary's, which was a credit to her imaginative powers; and that Ashe Park glowed like a stage setting in which she possessed sufficient self-consciousness to see herself as a player, a clever woman, unmarried but capable of responding to such spontaneous gatherings and sparking the evening by making clever remarks–all carefully counted and afterward relished.

Despite these rescued and dramatized social events, she must often have been impatient with the idle chatter of her country friends. We can easily imagine that a woman with such a well-stocked intelligence would have longed for more cerebral discourse than the price of ham and the newest fashion in bonnets, and probably she did. She is sure to have remembered how, years earlier, she and lively Tom Lefroy had sat in the parlor at Steventon and chattered openly about the novel *Tom Jones*. Two young people, they had read and responded to the same titillating passages. It may be that that tidemark of engaged conversation was never again matched—and that she forever after made do with smaller fare.

Nevertheless, her conversation about the cost and use of domestic items seems genuine, and appears to sit side by side with more abstract observations on moral behavior. And almost always when she spoke of the price of apples or of some small turn in fashion, she managed to coax a strain of irony into her remarks, a reminder to herself and others that she understood perfectly the discrepancy between ideas and objects. "You know how interesting the purchase of a sponge-cake is to me," she once wrote Cassandra, meaning that she was able to mock the very person she was, a clever woman who was, nonetheless, able to invest herself in tasks that others might find tedious.

There were always a few servants in the several households Jane Austen occupied, but never so many that the family escaped a share of domestic duties. She was probably ambivalent about such tasks, taking at least a minor pleasure in what she was obliged to do. Routine was essential to her creativity; the grounding in domestic reality was useful to her fiction and allowed her a wider range of understanding. She did complain on at least one occasion, though, much later at Chawton, that "Composition seems to me impossible with a head full of joints of mutton & doses of rhubarb." Her labor would have amounted to simple household sewing and to the planning of family meals and the ordering of supplies, not the actual acts of cooking, serving, or cleaning.

Economic restraint meant that she was locked into a quotidian life with its responsibilities for household management and that she was attached to a mixed community that bored her, amused her, and allowed her to be a full social being. More important, interaction with a large slice of society permitted her to observe and to gather material for her novels.

She often makes sharp remarks about her friends and speaks just slightly more obliquely about family members; almost everyone but Cassandra and her father suffered beneath her critical gaze. Her distinctions clearly entertain her or else she produces them to entertain others; she seems to have felt it an expression of her taste to criticize her neighbors for their fat necks and bad breath. She enjoys Miss Armstrong, the friend she met at Lyme Regis, but for the fact that she "seems to like people rather too easily."

It is in her comments about other people that she sometimes loses her footing between malice and wit, confusing irony with injury. The more lethal of these barbs appear in her letters to Cassandra and were perhaps designed to please an aspect of her sister's misanthropy that was otherwise hidden. Her novels espouse a far more generous appraisal of others. In *Emma* we read solemn and sensible advice that she herself often ignored: "It is very unfair to judge of any body's conduct, without an intimate knowledge of their situation.

Nobody, who has not been in the interior of a family, can say what the difficulties of any individual of that family may be."

Within the family, she felt genuine affection for Cassandra and for her brother Henry. What was it about Henry that endeared him to her? "Oh! what a Henry," she once said of him. Feckless is the term sometimes applied by others to his character: weak, unfocused. Of all the Austen brothers, it is Henry who appears to have lived the most hedonistically. James selected the church and stuck to it. Edward was plucked out to be a country gentleman and that was what he remained all his long life. Francis and Charles chose naval careers, where they thrived and were rewarded. Henry was educated for the church, sidestepped into the military, then became a banker, and, finally, following his bankruptcy, was ordained. His was a ring-around-the-rosy life, and it seems he took all his transformations with grace and with a lightness of heart. He married the woman he loved, his cousin Eliza de Feuillide, and after her death embarked on a second marriage. Constancy may not have been his strongest attribute, but he was constant, at least, in his love for his sister Jane. Only four years separated the two. His interests, like hers, were literary, and in an informal sense he acted as his sister's agent, beginning in 1803 with the submission to a publisher of *Northanger Abbey*. His pride in Jane's accomplishments was enormous. Made giddy by her success, he couldn't help but reveal her name to a public that had no idea who had authored her novels. In his moments of personal distress, he required Jane's presence, and perhaps it is this more than anything else that bound the two of them together. Interestingly, he is the only one of her brothers remembered in her will—with a bequest of £50.

Cassandra, sister and friend, is the most enigmatic presence in Jane Austen's life. Just two years apart, the only daughters in a family of brothers, they shared a bedroom all their lives; most of their time was spent together and, when separated, they corresponded with great frequency. Cassandra would have been the first reader of all Jane Austen's manuscripts, yet it was she who, out of prudence, recommended anonymity when the first novels were published. The younger sister always sought the favor of the older, always thinking of Cassandra's entertainment and satisfaction. It is hard not to see Cassandra's influence as infantilizing. Her sometimes cold critical comments about her sister's books (*Mansfield Park*, in particular) may have been inhibiting. The relationship with Cassandra sustained Jane Austen, but perhaps also damaged her impulses and self-trust.

Eliza Hancock (later Eliza de Feuillide and still later Eliza Austen) was an important friend. Her wit and worldliness brought continental freshness to the Austen circle of friends. She was an enthusiastic reader of Jane Austen's manuscripts and an encouraging presence, and it seems clear she preferred Jane to Cassandra.

Anne Lefroy may have lived the life of a conventional wife and mother, but her range of interests and her views were those of an independent consciousness. She had befriended the young Jane Austen eagerly after moving to the

Steventon area, lending her books and taking the young girl's writing seriously. The large difference in their ages was, curiously enough, not a barrier, and the friendship endured until Mrs. Lefroy's death, which occurred on Jane Austen's twenty-ninth birthday. The death was dramatic and shocking, a fall from a horse. Jane's grief at the loss may have been stirred by an old spoon of resentment, for it was Mrs. Lefroy who was partly responsible for separating her from young Tom Lefroy many years earlier. The anniversary of Mrs. Lefroy's death, occurring each year on Jane's birthday, must have poisoned the day. Four years after the fatal accident, perhaps in an attempt to exorcise her mingled feelings, she wrote a rhapsodic poem in Anne Lefroy's honor.

> I see her here, with all her smiles benign
> Her looks of eager love, her accents sweet;
> That voice and countenance almost divine;
> Expression, harmony, alike complete.
>
> Listen: 'tis not sound alone—'tis sense,
> 'Tis genius, taste and tenderness of soul:
> 'Tis genuine warmth of heart without pretence,
> And purity of mind that crowns the whole.

In her lifetime Jane Austen frequently declared her lack of respect for schoolteachers, but Anne Sharp, the governess to her nieces and nephews at Godmersham, was young, animated, and intelligent. The two women became friends, visiting and corresponding. "Dearest Anne," Austen addressed her, sharing with her the details of her life and expressing gratitude to her for her acts of friendship. Austen had enough respect for Miss Sharp to solicit her opinion about her later novels, *Mansfield Park* and *Emma*. Mrs. Elton was "beyond praise," Anne Sharp wrote, and this remark offers a comment on the sense of irony the two women shared: Mrs. Elton, as readers of *Emma* know, is undeserving of any praise at all, but Jane Austen's *drawing* of the egregious Mrs. Elton is a great accomplishment.

The Lloyd sisters, Mary and Martha, were old friends from Steventon days. Mary eventually married James Austen, becoming his second wife. Jane and Mary were never to be good friends, despite their closeness in age. The ten years between Martha and the younger Jane, however, did not diminish their very long friendship, first as neighbors and later as correspondents.

Some years later, when old Mrs. Lloyd had died, the Austen trio invited Martha to join their household. She remained with them in the following years–in Bath, Southampton, and finally, Chawton. She was an unmarried woman, without close family, and must have seemed to Jane and Cassandra another sister. She was welcomed for the congenial company she provided and no doubt for the financial help she may have contributed. At the age of sixty-three she became Francis Austen's second wife. By this time Jane Austen had been dead for years, but it is almost certain that she would have blessed the new arrangement and welcomed her old friend as a true Austen sister.

16

"SEVEN YEARS I suppose are enough to change every pore of one's skin and every feeling of one's mind." Jane Austen wrote these words to Cassandra in 1805, when she was thirty years old. She is speaking about the shift from country pleasures to the more elevated world of Bath society, but she might just as easily be addressing other major shifts in her life, periods in which she evolved from one being into another. Between the ages of eleven and eighteen she educated herself and began the long process of learning to write. And between the ages of eighteen and twenty-five she wrote three exuberant, confident novels. Seven or eight years of discouragement followed: the large family upheaval, the death of her father, pinched financial circumstances, and the realization that she was unlikely to marry and establish a home of her own. These were her difficult days, when she felt most keenly her lack of power over her own arrangements. She was not writing, and she had not yet convinced a publisher that she was a writer; in fact, she had scarcely tried.

The writing of three more great novels would follow, but she could not have known this at the age of thirty. What she may have felt, though, is that she was steadily humanizing herself, just as she had persisted in her course of self-education at Steventon Rectory. There was time, endless hours, in which to study the ways of society, at least that generous social slice that was offered to her. At an earlier age she had examined specimens through the lens of her father's microscope. Now she listened and observed the social noise that went on around her, all the time widening her range of human understanding. We don't know, step by step, the dimensions of her growing awareness, only that when the time came for her to pick up her pen once again at Chawton, she was ready. Her dramatic powers were fully in place and her moral vision of society was steady and focused.

Before the final move to Chawton, however, she was to endure a period of serious displacement. The lodgings in Bath were left behind in 1806, when Mrs. Austen took her daughters off on a long round of family visits before they settled in Southampton, where Francis and his wife Mary were living. A large, pleasant house was rented, but the Austen women found difficulty in establishing new friendships. Their residence was never more than tentative, and one or the other of the Austen sisters was always being called back to Steventon or to Godmersham to help out when a new baby arrived.

Finally, in 1808, when Jane was well into her thirties, her wealthy brother Edward stepped in at last to offer his mother and sisters a comfortable home. Why had he taken so long to attend to this responsibility? He may have been preoccupied with his enormous family and his business dealings. Or perhaps it was his wife, Elizabeth, who stood in his way–

Elizabeth had never been fond of Jane, finding her too clever to be good company. But Elizabeth was now dead, a collapse following the birth of her eleventh child. She was only thirty-five years old, the mother of an enormous family, much loved by her children, though viewed with some skepticism by her sister-in-law Jane.

Edward was a wealthy man, with many possibilities at his disposal. He gave his mother and sisters a choice. They might settle either in the attractive Kentish village of Wye, not far from Godmersham, or in a cottage in the Hampshire village of Chawton. Chawton, a village of about sixty families, was immediately selected; it stood in the beloved and familiar Hampshire landscape, and the cottage, at the juncture of three roads, could quickly be made ready for them. They would be only twelve miles from James and Mary at Steventon–this was very important to Mrs. Austen–and within easy walking distance from the town of Alton, where Henry often came on business.

Thousands of Jane Austen readers have by now visited Chawton Cottage, which is open to the public. Visitors divide their response down the middle; there are those who find the house surprisingly modest and located uncomfortably close to the busy road; others are astonished to find a "cottage" with six bedrooms, a garden, and some outbuildings. Architecturally it is a modest L-shaped affair, a two-storied house of red brick with sash windows and a tiled roof, which was already at least a hundred years old when the Austen party moved in. It may have been built as a small inn, but in the early nineteenth century it served as a home for Edward's bailiff, who had recently–conveniently–died.

A few improvements were made before the ladies arrived, mostly cleaning and decorating. Today's visitors are surprised to find that the front door opens directly into the dining room. The window of one of the sitting rooms faced the road but was blocked up before the Austen party moved in; this alteration, which was no doubt much discussed between Edward and his sisters, gives the house a somewhat blank, unbalanced look that is oddly charming in its asymmetry. A new, prettier window was installed overlooking the improved garden, a mixture of flowers, shrubs, grass, and orchard. Edward arranged for the planting of a hornbeam hedge between the house and road, thinking, probably, that it would protect the women from noise and dust. In fact, not one of them seems to have found the road a nuisance. The traffic, in fact, entertained them and made them feel in this isolated village that they were part of the ongoing world.

This would be Jane Austen's final home. Its importance to her was recognized by her nephew in his memoir; she had found a true home at last, whereas at Bath and Southampton she was "only a sojourner in a strange land."

Chawton made sense. It would be a relief to all the women to have a kinsman for a landlord. Edward would see that repairs were done promptly and that wood was provided for warmth. There would be no alarming rise in rents or leaky roof as there had been in Southampton. Edward Knight's name was a powerful one in the village, and this alone ensured that the household of women would be guaranteed respect. Two sitting rooms occupied the main floor, and the larger of these contained, once again, a piano for Jane, who played every morning before the other members of the family rose. The smaller sitting room was where she placed her writing table, and where most of her writing took place. The door to the room squeaked when anyone entered, and, according to legend, she specifically asked that the squeaking hinge go unoiled so that she would have notice of interruptions.

A narrow stairway, not in the least ostentatious, led to the second floor, where Martha Lloyd and Mrs. Austen each had a bedroom. Jane and Cassandra continued to share a bedroom; they were used to each other's company after so many years and had probably taken on some of the characteristics of long-settled couples: reading each other's thoughts and thinking along similar channels, accustomed to particular routines. A guest room was kept for visitors, and a good many visitors were anticipated, particularly the Austen brothers, who were always welcome. All these rooms were small, but each was adequately furnished in the rather simple style of country parsonages. Under Edward's eyes the garden was improved by the planting of trees and the construction of the sort of shrubbery walk that was considered suitable for women's exercise.

Helping to run the house were a cook, a housemaid, and a manservant. Mrs. Austen herself worked in the kitchen garden and, apparently, despite her bouts of poor health welcomed the outdoor exertions. Cassandra seems to have been the head of the house, looking after general housekeeping and accounts and management, with Jane responsible for organizing breakfast for the four women and for monitoring basic supplies of sugar, tea, and wine.

The possibility of achieving a settled state affected Jane Austen even before the actual move took place. Her spirits lifted; she felt emboldened, even silly with happiness. For her brother Francis, just a few days after the move, she composed a piece of cheerful doggerel, saluting the birth of his new son. Her own happiness leaps from the words.

> Our Chawton Home, how much we find
> Already in it, to our mind;
> And how convinced, that when complete
> It will all other Houses beat
> That ever have been made or mended,
> With rooms concise, or rooms distended.
> You'll find us very snug next year,
> Perhaps with Charles & Fanny near . . .

Snug, within the easy reach of an extended family, unworried about household expenses—all this brought Jane Austen's old spirits back. Months earlier, still stuck in Southampton but with Chawton in the future, she and Martha Lloyd attended the theater—there would be no theater near Chawton, as they well knew, and no amusements of the sort Bath had offered. None of this mattered. Austen was renewed, confident once again at the thought of the life she was about to inhabit.

Confident enough to write what has been called the famous MAD letter, MAD because she signed it with those initials, standing for Mrs. Ashton Dennis, a newly minted pseudonym. It is a name wittily designed to conceal and reveal her rage. Shortly before leaving Southampton in the spring of 1809, she sat down and composed a letter to the London publisher Crosby & Co. She had, after all, waited six years for a response concerning her manuscript. The tone is perfectly judged; she never abandons the outer boundaries of courtesy, but her intentions are lit with a blazing sense of injustice. Whatever anger she had stored up over the six-year wait was now poured out with finely tuned vitriol. She began with the deadly accurate narrative, followed by sly presumption, then boxed her enemy into a position of response–but never relinquished for a ladylike moment her sense of *politesse*. It was a letter worthy of Elizabeth Bennet in confrontation with Lady Catherine.

Wednesday 5 April 1809

Gentlemen

In the Spring of the year 1803 a MS Novel in 2 vol. Entitled Susan [*Northanger Abbey*] was sold to you by a Gentleman of the name of Seymour [Henry Austen's lawyer] & the purchase money £10 Rec/d at the same time. Six years have since passed, & this work of which I avow myself the Authoress, has never to the best of my knowledge, appeared in print, tho' an early publication was stipulated for at the time of Sale. I can only account for such an extraordinary circumstance by supposing the MS by some carelessness to have been lost; & if that was the case, am willing to supply You with another Copy if you are disposed to avail yourselves of it, & will engage for no further delay when it comes into your hands.–It will not be in my power from particular circumstances to command this Copy before the Month of August, but then, if you accept my proposal, you may depend on receiving it. Be so good as to send me a Line in answer, as soon as possible, as my stay in this place will not exceed a few days. Should no notice be taken of this Address, I shall feel myself at liberty to secure the publication of my work, by applying elsewhere. I am Gentlemen &c &c

MAD.–

Direct to M/rs Ashton Dennis
Post office, Southampton

It is impossible to miss the lightning bolts bouncing off the page. Jane Austen's outrage can be understood by any contemporary writer who has been treated in a disrespectful way by a publisher. Her own express helplessness, and the fact that she fully understood that helplessness, makes the situation particularly poignant.

Her letter was coolly dealt with by the publisher, who claimed never to have promised an immediate publication. They countered her threat of finding another publisher with their own: In fact, they stated that they would be ready to block with legal action any such attempt she might make. And—a particularly cruel suggestion—they offered to sell her manuscript back to her for the original £10.

She had no such amount at her disposal (her entire budget for the preceding year had been £50). She had been, it would seem, defeated by the professional, alien world of publishing. But the MAD letter, and its reply, which might have further maddened her, instead produced a ripe satisfaction. She had made her feelings known at last, and she was about to move to Chawton Cottage, in the midst of her beloved Hampshire, to surroundings that were sympathetic and calm, a refuge no less, where she would begin once again, picking up her pen and going forward in her life.

17

IT WASN'T UNTIL July of 1809 that the Austen party moved into Chawton Cottage. Events might have moved along more quickly, but Mrs. Austen, now seventy, had suffered a series of setbacks in her health, and these caused delay after delay. Several family visits intervened—to James and Mary at Steventon and to the grieving Knight family at Godmersham. Meanwhile, Chawton Cottage was being made ready. Repairs were completed under the supervision of Jane's brother Edward and included renovations to the water pump and back garden privy—which was all the family would have expected in the way of sanitation. Life at Chawton, as envisioned by the four women, was expected to be modest, even frugal. It was assumed that the family would grow and preserve some of their own food. They would exchange services with their neighbors, providing reading lessons for the village children in return for practical produce or labor. There would be no carriage for the ladies, but, in time, a donkey and donkey cart would become part of the Chawton household. Gentility, charm, order, and not extravagance, would rule the house.

Only one letter survives from Jane Austen's archives between 1809 and 1811, the congratulatory letter in verse to her brother Francis. This lack of correspondence does not point to a period of dead time, but rather to a settled period in which Jane Austen and her sister Cassandra were seldom separated. Routines were established in these early years at Chawton, and it was routine that Jane Austen loved. The immediate neighbors in the region may not have known how the spinster Jane Austen occupied her days, but the other women of the household did, and they accommodated the schedule it demanded.

After a session at the piano, and after organizing the family breakfast, Jane Austen settled down to her writing in the smaller of the two sitting rooms. Dinner, the main meal of the day, was served between three and four-thirty in the afternoon. After that would come the social part of the day: conversation, card games, and still later, tea. The evening was often spent reading aloud from novels, and probably it was during this time that Jane read her ongoing work to her audience of intimates. She was famous for her readings, if we can believe her brother Henry, which were always delivered with a sense of drama. "She read aloud with very great taste and effect," said Henry in the biographical notice that accompanied the publication of *Northanger Abbey* shortly after her death.

She was both lucky and unlucky. Lucky because she had a trusted audience with a wide range of taste—her mother, her old friend Martha Lloyd, Cassandra, other visiting siblings who were passing through, and old friends—all of whom had known her since girlhood and had witnessed her developing skills as a novelist. This coterie was knowledgeable about what caught her author's eye, those moments of moral inaction, the premises that would make or undo a woman's life. They knew her successes (the spirited, satisfying rondure of *Pride and Prejudice*) and her failures (the ugly and narratively misshapen *Lady Susan*). They were not a spontaneous, anonymous audience, but an engaged and humanly bonded readership (listening perhaps rather than actually reading) who had traveled every inch of the way with Jane Austen as she had lived her life and discovered her own writerly process. They were, in fact, part of that complicated process; they understood its hesitations and welcomed its revivals. And, more important, they were sympathetic, a readerly perspective that goes beyond being merely encouraging. They may not have been writers themselves, but they understood to a certain extent the gathering and accretion of Jane Austen's skill with dialogue, with description and with moral exegesis. She was their sister, daughter, friend, neighbor, not some anonymous writer whose works were borrowed or bought; her struggle belonged at least partly to them–certainly it was known to them. Their personal affection for her made them in many ways an ideal audience; their attachment to the novel form, which was still evolving in the early years of the nineteenth century and which would continue to evolve, gave them a particular credibility. They–her friends, her family–were critically alert, and at the same time emotionally attuned. Writing is in the end a solitary pursuit, but

Jane Austen's novels were written and revised in concert with a remarkable communal consultation. This was part of her good luck.

Her bad luck was that she was enclosed all her life by obscurity. Just as she walked behind a wall of shrubbery at Steventon and later at Chawton, she wrote her novels behind a wall of isolation. Sympathetic readers are one thing, but writers are hugely dependent on the shared experiences of other writers. Why otherwise do we have such an empire of writers' colonies, writers' unions, writers' congresses, writers' guilds? Writers uphold and defend each other with discussion of their difficulties—this has always been the case—and persuade each other that their individual endeavors, which often seem no more substantial than paper airplanes tossed into the uninterested air, are not egotistical projections, not valueless streams of indulgence, but contributions (what a pompous word that seems!) to an ongoing civil discourse. Writers can also, of course, be jealous and destructive of one another's efforts, but their shared presence, their friendships and correspondence, always serve notice that writing is valued in a community, and is far from the insane and solitary act it may appear to be.

Jane Austen's nephew James Edward Austen-Leigh got a number of things wrong in his aunt's biography, but he understood the ways in which she might have suffered.

Jane Austen lived in entire seclusion from the literary world; neither by correspondence, nor by personal intercourse was she known to any contemporary authors. It is probable that she never was in company with any contemporary authors. It is probable that she never was in company with any persons whose talents or whose celebrity equaled her own; so that her powers never could have been sharpened by collision with superior intellects, nor her imagination aided by their casual suggestions. Whatever she produced was a home-made article.

The term "home-made article" is a phrase of great originality, an inspired piece of terminology. The novel as a home-made article—what does this mean? Art can be described as "making." We may think of novelists, in postmodernist terms, as workers who are remaking, revising, reinventing, but novelists in Jane Austen's era were working at an even sterner forge, where the dimensions of fictional belief and disbelief were being examined: How does a writer extract from real life those components that describe and interrogate "life" without pretending to be a replication? How does the writer signal to the reader that a novel's fictional skin is something other than reportage? By how many degrees is mimetic art separated from the seen, felt, and heard field of our own being? How closely do we desire an overlapping of the real and the projected? Not at all? Or do we want to be persuaded that fictional truth is congruent with what we know, what we have already heard and accepted?

A home-made article, Jane Austen's nephew had called

his aunt's work. Her novels were conceived and composed in isolation. She invented their characters, their scenes and scenery, and their moral framework. The novelistic architecture may have been borrowed from the eighteenth-century novelists, but she made it new, clean, and rational, just as though she'd taken a broom to the old fussiness of plot and action. She did all this alone.

"Even during the last two or three years of her life, when her works were rising in the estimation of the public, they did not enlarge the circle of her acquaintance"–so wrote her nephew, who must have guessed what a deprivation this was to his aunt. She would have relished the company of other novelists. And she might have been comforted and encouraged to know something about the universal difficulty of transmuting the real to the fictional. Such shared insights would have softened her gaze and might have widened her level of tolerance. Instead she was forced to go it alone, working out her compromises in the light of her own confined knowledge.

Once settled at Chawton, she went back to her old manuscripts–by then she must have considered them old friends. She even pulled out the notebooks she'd written in her youth and emended a few passages. Contentedly, or so it seems, she unpacked the heaped pages she had written some ten years earlier and began a series of revisions. *First Impressions,* the family favorite, later known as *Pride and Prejudice,* was lightly edited during the months following the move to

Chawton; *Sense and Sensibility* may have received more in the way of revision—it was, in any case, the first of the manuscripts she sent to a publisher.

Brother Henry, from London, was advising her to send a copy of *Sense and Sensibility* to a publisher (Egerton's of Whitehall) whom he had contacted. She had another look at the novel, and brought one or two minor references up to date: the institution of the twopenny post and the mention of Walter Scott as a reigning literary light. After that the manuscript was dispatched.

Late in the year 1810 she received word that the novel had been accepted for publication. Her jubilation was surely tempered by the fact that the publisher had accepted this first manuscript by an unknown writer "on commission." This meant that it would be printed at the author's own expense, and she would be expected to take up the loss if the sale of copies failed to repay the expense of publication.

She was cautious in matters of economy. Her circumstances demanded that she weigh every penny. But, with money borrowed from Henry and Eliza, she seems not to have hesitated for a moment about jumping into the venture. She knew, perhaps, the worth of the manuscript, that it would draw readers as it had delighted her family. And besides, she might not have another chance. This was it.

18

THE DIFFERENCE between a published and unpublished author is enormous, and every novelist in the world would agree: *It is a truth universally acknowledged* that published authors, even those whose books have not yet appeared before the public, are filled with a new and reckless confidence in their own powers.

Jane Austen, thirty-six years old, traveled to London in March of 1811 so that she could work at correcting the proofs of *Sense and Sensibility*. The very phrase "correcting proofs" must have excited her imagination. She stayed in the Sloane Street house of Henry and Eliza, who drew her into a whirl of theatergoing and parties, galleries and museums, and modest shopping for printed muslin, which she characterized as "extravagant." Her letters to Cassandra during the next two months are close to being feverish. She bubbles with happiness, with stray thoughts, with gossip. "I have so many little matters to tell you of, that I cannot wait any longer before I begin to put them down." Everything she sees delights her. Everyone she meets is sympathetically drawn. At a large and elegant party given by Henry and Eliza, she says, "We were all delight & cordiality of course."

Cassandra must have written to ask whether, amid all the social comings and goings, she was giving much thought to the publication of *Sense and Sensibility*. Her tone may well have been scolding, or at least chiding. Jane replied, "No indeed, I am never too busy to think of S&S. I can no more forget it, than a mother can forget her sucking [sic] child." And then she adds, as though to placate Cassandra, "I am much obliged to you for your enquiries." She had by then just two more sheets to correct and was hoping for a June publication.

In fact, it would be late October before the *Morning Chronicle* announced "a New Novel by a Lady–." Something like one thousand copies were printed, selling for 15 shillings. An article in the *Critical Review* (1812) deemed, in a rather low-key voice, that "the incidents are probable, and highly pleasing, and interesting; the conclusion such as the reader must wish it should be, and the whole is just long enough to interest without fatiguing."

The book sold well. Jane Austen's anonymity was preserved, even for a time from family members. It is Cassandra, rather than Jane, who seems to have encouraged this secrecy, but the subterfuge was one that both of them enjoyed and that they made into something of a game. James and Mary at Steventon were at last let into the conspiracy, and James, Jane's least favorite brother, sent her a poem of praise, signed simply "A Friend." It was written in a disguised hand and ended with the encouraging lines:

O then, gentle lady! Continue to write,
And the sense of your reader t'amuse & delight.

James was often considered the writer of the family, at least
by Cassandra, though his verses remained unpublished. But
success can breed good will, even in families, and besides, the
tables had been turned; now his younger sister Jane was being recognized and, in a strictly anonymous way, celebrated.

The publisher Egerton wrote to say that all the first edition copies had been sold. Tucked into the postscript of a letter to her brother Francis, Jane Austen exclaims, as though
she can hardly help herself, "There is to be a 2/d Edition to
S&S. Egerton advises it." A sense of jubilation accompanies
this piece of information, and there is the sense, too, that she
is trying with all her might to keep a cap on her satisfaction
by sprinkling her letters with other more mundane references: deaths, babies, the weather, the scarcity of apples, her
mother's headaches. Her efforts don't quite succeed. Her joy
in publication keeps breaking through. This, it would seem,
is what she had always wanted; she may have missed out on
marriage and motherhood, and certainly she had been denied the financial means to a life of independence. But she
was a writer of genius, as she must have known, and that genius was now, in a very small way, being recognized and applauded. A second sweet source of happiness must have
been that her own family—where she was the younger sister,
a little eccentric and strange—was made aware of her gifts.

After a period of scant correspondence, there is an out-pouring of letters. It is well known that Cassandra destroyed those letters that she felt reflected poorly on Jane, and per-haps poorly on herself and other family members. What was it in particular that caught Cassandra's censor's eye? Imme-diately before the publication of *Sense and Sensibility,* Jane Austen's letters were particularly astringent. She niggled at neighbors; her gossip had a poisonous pitch; her last attempt at writing, *The Watsons,* was a book with a bleak horizon and a host of embittered women. There are only a handful of these surviving letters, and it can be imagined that Cassandra was anxious to extirpate this unattractive side of her sister's expression. Overnight, with the appearance of Jane Austen's first published novel and her buoyant new spirit, there are streams of letters sparkling with happiness, animated, deter-minedly distracted, breathless.

Nevertheless, publication meant having a public self after a life that had been austerely private. Her scale of values, her opinions were now being read by a wide public, and not just received by the family circle. The two selves, public and pri-vate, were in danger of flying apart, but her correspondence shows her efforts to hang on to all that was familiar while en-joying the titillation of celebrity.

She had earned, to her great astonishment, well over £100. This was the only money she had ever earned by her pen other than the £10 put forward years earlier for *Northanger Abbey,* which still lay unpublished. Now she had money for small gifts, mostly for Cassandra, and money to pay for her own travels to London and back.

At once she set about correcting the manuscript for *Pride and Prejudice*. "I have lopt & cropt so successfully . . . that I imagine it must be rather shorter than S&S." *Pride and Prejudice* had always been the family favorite, and she herself loved the character of Elizabeth Bennet. "I must confess that *I* think her as delightful a creature as ever appeared in print, & how I shall be able to tolerate those who do not like *her* at least, I do not know." This ebullient faith in her next published novel was unrestrained, and already she was planning a new novel, which, she said, would be about a wholly different subject, ordination. This projected novel was to be *Mansfield Park*.

Full of new confidence, she was also becoming more critical of her own work. She could afford to be, now that she had readers who admired her and bought her books. Of *Pride and Prejudice* she said, "The work is rather too light & bright & sparkling;–it wants shade;–it wants to be stretched out here & there with a long Chapter . . . about something unconnected with the story; an Essay on Writing, a critique on Walter Scott, or the history of Buonaparte [sic]–or anything that would form a contrast & bring the reader with increased delight to the playfulness & Epigrammatism of the general stile." She doubted, she said, whether Cassandra, with her "starched Notions," would agree, and it may be she was seeking confirmation. Whether we have Cassandra to thank or Jane Austen's own sound critical judgment, there was no added material to pad out the novel and provide "shade" and no sideways essays on the matter of composition. Her publisher Egerton offered £110 for the copyright, which meant that this time around Henry was not obliged to advance money for printing costs. The book sold for 18 shillings and was once again published anonymously, advertised as being by the author of *Sense and Sensibility.* "I want to tell you that I have got my own darling Child from London," she wrote Cassandra when a finished copy of *Pride and Prejudice* arrived at Chawton in late January of 1813. Like all newly published writers, she may have magnified its potential effect. She was pleased Cassandra was away at the time, she said, because "it might be unpleasant to you to be in the Neighbourhood at the first burst of the business." What business? It is not clear why publication might have embarrassed or discomfited Cassandra; Jane Austen was being disingenuous, or else she was acting out of her lifetime habit of deferring to her older sister. In fact, she was disappointed that Cassandra was away at a moment of celebration, and worried that her sister, in fact, might have deliberately absented herself. The only celebration of the new "child" consisted of a reading out loud of the novel with her mother and a neighbor at Chawton. Her mother read badly, and this soured what pleasure Jane Austen felt in the occasion. She longed for her family's proud cries of approval. Her second novel was in print, a novel sought after by her publisher and purchased with a reasonable advance. There should have been a celebration party of friends and family, and the bright atmosphere of adulatory toasts. Instead, on a winter's night, she was confined at Chawton Cottage, seated by the fire, hearing her words mumbled with inappropriate rhythms and emphasis.

The book met with immediate success. Readers loved it, laughed at it, were moved by it, and they adored especially the vibrancy and spirit of Elizabeth Bennet. "*Pride and Prejudice* rises very superior to any novel we have lately met with in the delineation of domestic scenes," said the *Critical Review.* "Nor is there one character which appears flat, or obtrudes itself upon the notice of the reader with troublesome impertinence."

Her delight in the novel's immediate success coincided with an uneasy time with Cassandra. Jane found herself always in the position of propitiating her sister, and trying to keep control of her own exultation. Instead of taking pleasure in the book's reception, she committed herself to a fussy displeasure about the typographical errors that had cropped up. It would be selfish, she must have reasoned, to rejoice in the satisfaction she felt. Others would condemn her self-cherishing thoughts and remarks. The situation was untenable. She must not seem to be too happy. But she was.

19

SHE TOOK REFUGE in knowing she had a new novel on the boil. And *Mansfield Park* was, for her, a leap into new fictional space, and perhaps even an act of redress for the lack of "shade" in her previous two novels; now she must be serious; now she must mute her natural irony and deal with the subject of goodness and virtue.

The characters in this novel, the self-satisfied, entitled inhabitants of Mansfield Park, move through the daily patterns they have come to enjoy and never suspect, even as the narrative skies darken, that the house is about to come tumbling down. It collapses catastrophically, spreading circles of damage everywhere, leaving at the center Fanny Price and the reader's wish that Fanny might, just once, recognize her priggishness.

The novel does not exhilarate as *Pride and Prejudice* does, nor does it dramatize in the same way that *Sense and Sensibility* does. It is solid—perhaps too solid—morally bewildering, and certainly perplexing to a contemporary audience. Its heroine, Fanny Price, is largely responsible for the difficulty of the novel.

What is the matter with Fanny Price, shadow heroine of

Mansfield Park? Why is she so dutiful, passive, lacking in spirit, so relentlessly correct, so given—when she is invited—to little puffs of sanctimoniousness, and why, despite these qualities, does she end up the respected mistress of the Bertram family and their worthy country seat, Mansfield Park? No one, to use one of Jane Austen's favorite words, is more "particular" than Fanny. Where Fanny's finely attuned moral sense comes from is something of a mystery, a triumph over both genetics and environment.

The question of Fanny has teased the readers of Jane Austen's novels for close to two centuries. Austen's other heroines possess spirit and wit. In their youth and exuberance they are sometimes impolite, rash, imprudent, mistaken in their judgment. Emma Woodhouse lacks maturity and tact. Elizabeth Bennet hurls herself blindly at life. Catherine of *Northanger Abbey* is helplessly curious. *Persuasion*'s Anne Elliot, Fanny Price's closest sister in the oeuvre, is easily led but at the same time innately wise and always supported by an inner assurance.

Not one of these heroines, though, has begun life as radically disentitled as Fanny Price of Portsmouth, and in the reading and understanding of her character, some of our contemporary psychological insights can be brought into view. A sensitive child, Fanny spends the first decade of her life with a rough drinker for a father and a slatternly mother who prefers her sons to her daughters. Abruptly, and without her consultation, she is plucked from this disorderly home and placed in elegant Mansfield Park, where she meets with one indolent aunt, a second aunt who is cruelly manipulative, an absentee uncle, and a set of cousins who have every advantage over her. Here she is reminded daily that she is inferior to the members of the Bertram family and that she must be grateful for the crumbs that fall her way. She is called upon to perform dull and unrewarding services, and when she reaches womanhood, she is subjected to the pressing attentions of one Henry Crawford, a man she loathes.

Her rejection of this match brings upon her the wrath of the Bertram family and a punishing banishment back to her own family in Portsmouth, where she is powerless, virtually without funds, and kept ignorant of her future. That this pattern of abuse has created a being as repressed as Fanny is not in the least surprising. The modern reader understands precisely why Fanny is Fanny. Hers is a case of the Cinderella syndrome, of the prisoner's self-protective strategy. Her weakness is close to being a debility, an illness, but one that confers on her the crown of moral superiority. She is enfeebled in somewhat the same way Christian saints are sometimes portrayed, possessing bodies that are too ephemeral for this world, separated from the main, ruddy, healthy stream. Mary Crawford asks at one point whether Fanny is "out"? Meaning, has she been presented to society? Well, no. Her reticence, her withdrawal, is fueled by a curious stubbornness of the soul. Her spirit urges her to be "in," not "out." The problem is, Can the reader love her?

Austen clearly does love her. "My Fanny," she calls her in the novel's remarkable final chapter, in which all the narrative lines are brought to conclusion and the whole cast of characters summed up. Fanny triumphs in the end partly because Austen has artfully cleared the field for her: The two Bertram sisters are in disgrace; Aunt Norris has been sent packing; Mary Crawford, Fanny's rival in love, has been exposed in her moral shallowness. Fanny's uncle, Sir Thomas, humiliated and lost, requires the consolation of a daughter he can trust, and Fanny stands ready to fulfill that role. She is, as always, available. Furthermore, Austen has put the reader in a near impossible situation, for if we underrate Fanny's essential value, we put ourselves in the same camp as the Bertrams.

But Fanny does have real claims on our attention, despite her joylessness. She shows growing signs of independent thought—her little discourse, for instance, on memory in chapter 22. "There seems something more speakingly incomprehensible in the powers, the failures, the inequalities of memory, than in any other of our intelligences." She is, in fact, quite silent for the first half of the novel, then bursts into a promising articulation in the second half. And she becomes capable of anger—about time!—in chapter 33 when the obdurate Henry Crawford refuses to believe she cannot love him. ("Now she was angry," Austen says plainly.)

And, most particularly, we can esteem Fanny's resourcefulness when she is returned to her awful Portsmouth family. There she brings order where she can, assisting one of her brothers in his departure and introducing a sister, Susan, to the pleasures of literature. She saves Susan, in fact, by bringing her to Mansfield Park, where her life will be greatly improved. It is this instance of the helpless coming to the rescue of the even more tragically helpless that wins our hearts and convinces us, once again, that Austen has read all the signs and correctly apportioned the rewards.

Mansfield Park, in three volumes, selling for 18 shillings, was published in the spring of 1814, and its author was identified only as the same Lady who had written *Sense and Sensibility* and *Pride and Prejudice*. Silence followed, though Jane Austen searched diligently for reviews. A parallel blow of silence came from her family, and she began to suspect they disliked the novel or else were already accustomed to her publications—there goes Aunt Jane again with one of her novels!

In fact, there were other distractions. Edward Knight was fighting a legal battle over his land holdings. And the wars in Europe had been heating up. France had been invaded by Prussia, Russia, and Austria, and the British forces under Wellington crossed the Pyrenees, heading north. A mere month or so before the publication of *Mansfield Park*, Napoléon was exiled to the island of Elba. Not surprisingly, the buzz of conversation at Chawton concerned events other than the publication of a maiden aunt's third novel, which was, though no one said so directly, not quite up to the spirit of the previous two. The book was conservative in a time of reckless change, allowing the traditional values of reflection to win over the modish and stylish excitement represented by Henry and Mary Crawford. It is an awkward novel to appreciate in our own times; even in its original year of publication it must have seemed easy to overlook.

Novelists, though, tend to be solipsistic, especially in the fragile days immediately following publication. Austen decided on the somewhat humiliating idea of collecting the opinions of family and friends and copying these into a notebook titled "Opinions of Mansfield Park."

Her brother Francis observed that "Fanny is a delightful Character!" and he very much admired his sister's handling of the character of Aunt Norris, who is one of the evil women of literature, almost too wicked to be amusing, a bully and sycophant who is satisfyingly punished in the course of the novel. "You need not fear," said Francis, "the publication being discreditable to the talents of it's [sic] author." Mrs. Austen found Fanny "insipid." Jane's two favorite nieces, Anna and Fanny, were divided on the subject of Fanny Price; Anna couldn't abide her, but Fanny professed admiration. Without a doubt it was Cassandra's opinion that mattered the most, and hers survives, on paper anyway, as rather chilly: It was "quite as clever, tho' not so brilliant" as *Pride and Prejudice.* Henry resorted to the phrase that all squirming and dissatisfied readers use when speaking to an author about her work: The novel, he said, was "extremely interesting." Even contemporary novelists feel the pain, and subtext, of that particular coded message, "extremely interesting." Henry's wife Eliza had died a year earlier—probably from breast cancer—and perhaps he was not in a mood to concentrate on what his sister's book accomplishes so marvelously: the handling of its large cast of characters, its sense of theatrical expansiveness, and its brave exploration of social injustice.

Austen quotes (a little desperately) a friend, Mr. Cooke, who claims *Mansfield Park* to be "the most sensible Novel he ever read." Her anxious seeking of opinions concerning her novel, and her careful recording of them, gesture toward her own uneasiness with what she had written. She had intended to write about the subject of church ordination, and yet the novel slides away from that subject more often than toward it. It is a novel about belonging and not belonging, about love between siblings, about fine gradations of morality, and, ultimately, about human noise and silence, action and stillness.

Clearly she was disappointed in its reception. But she was already doing what any discouraged novelist does: She was beginning a new novel, *Emma*, which was to be a masterpiece.

20

READERS OF *Emma* like to remind themselves that this is the novel in which we hear the remarkable line: "One half of the world cannot understand the pleasure of the other." There are readers who are unable to understand the appeal of *Emma,* and even its appreciators may feel trapped in a discussion in which Emma Woodhouse is declared to be a rich, rather nasty spoiled brat, Mr. Woodhouse a bit over the top, Mr. Knightley a cold potato who is not as sexy as Mr. Darcy of *Pride and Prejudice,* and the whole Jane Fairfax/Frank Churchill plot a rather clumsy appendage that never quite gets brought to life. All this is true, and the reader also remembers Jane Austen's own concern about Emma herself: that no one would love this young woman the way she, Emma's creator, loved her.

In this novel, more than any of the others, readers tend to focus on the single most important character rather than on the architecture of the novel–always a problem with Jane Austen criticism. Emma is a puzzle: rich, beautiful, and delighted to be Miss Woodhouse, the unchallenged leader of Highbury society. Other than possessing a boldness of temperament and a sanguine nature, her natural abilities are not obvious. She is not gifted musically. Her drawing, her ability to produce a likeness, is poor; she admits as much. She is not a serious or disciplined reader, even though Mr. Knightley provides her with lists of improving books he hopes she will read.

Well, what is she good at? She is good at observing the people around her, although she makes great, gulping mistakes, as we know. And she is gifted at devising other, alternate arrangements for people; she is occupied, obsessed, with rupturing and amending other people's affection, for instance. Exuberant, ever inventive, she runs a number of plot lines simultaneously and allows them to cross and recross. Following the gypsy scene in which her friend Harriet is badly frightened, she describes herself as being an "imaginist," a word not found in modern dictionaries, on fire with "speculation and foresight." She is, in short, a novelist, for these interfering and manipulative acts are what novelists busy themselves with. She may not have actually sat down to write a novel, but as a character she plays up and down the novelist's keyboard and perhaps even adds a few new notes, top and bottom.

Emma is a young twenty-one, and she is the only Austen heroine to be independently wealthy. There are those who call *Emma,* like *Northanger Abbey,* a coming-of-age novel, and it is plain that young Miss Woodhouse does experience a growth in self-awareness. Under the forgiving guidance of her surrogate mother, Mrs. Weston, and of the ever present Mr. Knightley, she comes to recognize her acts of insensitiv-

ity to Miss Bates, her coldness to Jane Fairfax, her manipulative behavior toward Harriet, and her social misjudgment
concerning Robert Martin and his family. She also sees at last
what we, the readers, have seen all along, that which lies just
beneath her nose—that Mr. Knightley is the man, the only
man, she can love and that he loves her in return. She has
found her home in the world at last.

Mr. Knightley, like all Jane Austen's heroes, is a reading
man, and this alone would tip off any reader almost at once
as to what his ultimate role will be. Despite knowing this, or
rather because of knowing it, the reader experiences a kind of
shiver every time George Knightley walks out on the page.
(The deep, deep seriousness and the perfect judgment that
characterize him make it seem just a little cheeky to call him
George, and in fact Emma, even after accepting his marriage
proposal, announces that she has no intention of doing so.)

There are those who say that Emma married the father
she should have had, and it is true that most contemporary
readers would find it hard to imagine the pillow talk the two
of them are to enjoy in their married life. He is much older,
so much wiser, and has known her since childhood. His eye
for character is exact—as hers is not—and this tells us something about what Jane Austen may have felt about the novelistic eye for character, which is often misguided, more
forgiving, or else more easily affronted than "real" appraisals.
Emma was not so much attracted by Frank Churchill as distracted by him, but Mr. Knightley saw straight to the truth:
that Frank was "a man who seemed to love without feeling,"

a comment that at the same time throws our notions of love *and* feeling up into the air.

Emma's advancement in self-understanding is accompanied by a growth of her rational side, and we see this most clearly in the moment when Mr. Knightley–George–makes his declaration of love. Listening to his ardent words, Emma becomes "almost ready to sink under the agitation of this moment." Almost, Jane Austen writes, but not quite. We are told that "while he spoke, Emma's mind was most busy." Even while continuing to take in every word Mr. Knightley utters, she is at the same time rapidly inventorying the situation: one, rejoicing in her lover's ardor; two, adding up Harriet's disappointment; and, three, congratulating herself on not having given away Harriet's secret. In short, she is busy as any accountant, calculating the balance of fortune and misfortune. As for Mr. Knightley, he is made happy that Emma is his "by hand and word," a sentiment that may strike a modern reader as being decidedly more chilly than "body and soul." But after setting aside the legalistic interpretation of "hand and word," the two phrases may roughly correspond.

When Jane Austen wrote *Emma* she had already received public encouragement–and a certain measure of discouragement, too–with the reception of *Mansfield Park*. *Emma* shows a self-assuredness that comes straight at the reader's consciousness, and we see Jane Austen's own concentration of pleasure in her powers. The fusing of moral consideration and human drama achieves perfect pitch.

The novel is rich in comedy, too. Mrs. Elton, silly and snobbish, is captured with all her flaws when she attends a strawberry-picking party hosted by Mr. Knightley. Mrs. Elton, Jane Austen writes, appears in "all her apparatus of happiness"—and what an extraordinary phrase this is: *apparatus of happiness.* She leads the way with her bonnet and basket and gives voice to her exuberance. We don't quite know to whom she is addressing her scattered, telescoped remarks— to the wind, perhaps, or to readers who can feel Jane Austen winking in their direction. "The best fruit in England— everybody's favourite—always wholesome.—These the finest beds and finest sorts.—Delightful to gather for one's self—the only way of really enjoying them.—Morning decidedly the best time—never tired—every sort good—hautboy infinitely superior—no comparison—the others hardly eatable—hautboys very scarce—Chili preferred—white wood finest flavour of all—price of strawberries in London—abundance about Bristol—Maple Grove—cultivation—beds when to be renewed—gardeners never to be put out of their way—delicious fruit—only too rich to be eaten much of—inferior to cherries— currants more refreshing—only objection to gathering strawberries the stooping—glaring sun—tired to death—could bear it no longer—must go and sit in the shade."

21

By 1815 Jane Austen's anonymity was breaking down at last and leading to a minor degree of celebrity. A great many people now knew the name of the author of *Pride and Prejudice* and *Mansfield Park*. At first only a few intimates had been told the truth of authorship; after that it was not surprising that these few told a few more. Henry Austen, proud brother of the author, bursting with reflected happiness, was incapable of discretion, even though he had been cautioned more than once.

There is every indication that Jane Austen enjoyed her new fame. And the financial reward that went with it. *Mansfield Park* had sold out, despite its quiet reception. *Pride and Prejudice*, the perennial favorite, was in its third edition, and *Sense and Sensibility* in its second. Admirers were everywhere, including the Prince Regent, who let it be known that he would be honored if Jane Austen were to dedicate her next volume to him. *Emma* was published in 1816, once again anonymously, but carrying the royal dedication:

TO

HIS ROYAL HIGHNESS

THE PRINCE REGENT

THIS WORK IS,
BY HIS ROYAL HIGHNESS'S PERMISSION,
MOST RESPECTFULLY
DEDICATED,
BY HIS ROYAL HIGHNESS'S
DUTIFUL
AND OBEDIENT
HUMBLE SERVANT,
THE AUTHOR.

The effusive dedication was not Jane Austen's idea; she had something much simpler in mind, but she was advised that the correct form must be used, that there was no choice in the matter. Moreover, royal "suggestions" must be taken as seriously as commands.

The publisher, Egerton, had postponed a second edition of *Mansfield Park,* and the frustrated Jane Austen threw up her hands and found a new publisher, John Murray. Murray, with the encouragement of the Prince Regent's dedication, published two thousand copies of *Emma,* more than Jane Austen had ever seen come off the press. She may have been embarrassed by the royal advertisement, particularly when her friend Martha Lloyd teased her about mercenary motives, but she was not at all naïve about what a royal stamp of approval would do for her. The unmarried daughter of a vicar, without money or connections, she had become linked to another world where rewards of all kinds were promised.

Once again she was anxious about how her immediate circle received the book. Charles, her youngest brother, loved *Emma* and read the novel three times in quick succession. Other family members, when quizzed, placed it in a limbo between the preceding novels, and Miss Anne Sharp, Jane's schoolteacher friend, pointed out the weakness of the Jane Fairfax plot. There was a small stir of objection to her characterization of the clergy: The ridiculing of Mr. Elton was almost as objectionable as that directed at Mr. Collins. The great Walter Scott was approached by the publisher for an opinion, which he delivered without real enthusiasm. A few years later he reversed the coolness of his thoughts about the novelist Jane Austen, writing in his diary, "That young lady had a talent for describing the involvements and feelings and characters of ordinary life, which is to me the most wonderful I have ever met with. The Big Bow-Wow strain I can do myself like any now going; but the exquisite touch which renders ordinary common-place things and characters interesting from the truth of the description and the sentiment is denied to me."

Jane Austen had been dead for many years by the time Scott's words were made public. But such praise, coming as it did from the great "Bow-Wow" novelist himself, guaranteed her a readership in the nineteenth century, and his praise is still called up today to demonstrate how Austen was valued in her own time, if only by a few. The words would have meant much more to her than the tenuous association with the Prince Regent; she was never, in fact, persuaded that His Highness actually read *Emma* or had any notion of her "exquisite touch."

22

ANNE ELLIOT OF *Persuasion* is twenty-seven years old as the novel opens, making her the oldest of Jane Austen's heroines. She has been grievously injured by a broken engagement, and she is past her "bloom"–a favorite word of Jane Austen–meaning that the blood-filled elasticity of good health has deserted her, and so has the hope of a fuller life to come. She is living, most unhappily, with her own error, her decision some years earlier to break her engagement to the naval officer Frederick Wentworth: He was poor; he would have to make his own way; he was not a good marital risk. But he has returned to the neighborhood as the novel opens. Eight and a half years have passed, and he has become successful in his career and much admired. Resentment lingers with him, until he finds Anne Elliot in a state of being only half alive. Her "mistake" in rejecting him has conferred on her the role of maiden aunt, a condition she does not relish. She is emotionally detached from everyone in her family and looking forward to a life of disappointment.

She might easily have shared the blame for her young disaster with Lady Russell, her surrogate mother, who persuaded the young Anne that Wentworth would not be an ideal husband. But Lady Russell does not fall easily into the category of the wicked stepmother, just as Anne does not belong to the company of the easily led. *Persuasion* may have structural faults as a novel, but it is a grown-up book whose characters are alive in their ambiguity. Part of Captain Wentworth's charm—and he is a most nimble-minded, intelligent hero—is his ability to shift his perspective. Like Anne, he has been bruised by rejection, but not fatally injured or made blind. The dance between them is one of reassessment and maturity. They listen to each other's words, observe each other's actions, and are particularly watchful for small gestures and suggestions.

Jane Austen was forty when she was working on *The Elliots,* as *Persuasion* was initially titled. She wrote it relatively quickly and then revised the conclusion by substituting a new chapter twenty-two and twenty-three. This alteration, really a critique of her own novelistic sense, puts a torque on the whole narrative, illuminating both Anne and Captain Wentworth and the nature of their renewed love. Women have a second chance in this narrative of love everlasting; it is never too late to revise and reclaim the past.

The original ending lacks tension and drama. Anne and Wentworth are alone in a room; they refer briefly to a misunderstanding, which Anne quickly clears up, leaving an opening for Wentworth to press his suit, which she quickly accepts. The scene feels both abrupt and contrived. The amended ending, on the other hand, takes place in a crowded room, and is one of the most famous scenes in literature. In this version Anne is allowed an active rather than passive role. She enters into a spirited discussion with her friend Captain Harville about the different expectations of men and women and the tactics the two sexes must employ. Captain Harville reminds her of the inconstancy of women, how the theme of such inconstancy is so pervasive in literature that it must be true. Anne protests, refusing the wisdom of books that are of course written by men. "All the privilege I claim," she cries, "is that of loving longest, when existence or when hope is gone."

Anne becomes aware that Captain Wentworth, sitting nearby and writing a letter, has heard every word. He picks up his pen again and writes to Anne, pleading his love and assuring her that his affection has not diminished even after eight and a half years. The scene becomes a ballet of glances given and received, of understandings reached not directly but through a look, a gesture, and the unspoken subtext of all that has been said aloud. These two lovers are not shown in an unreal isolation as in the original ending, but are clearly part of the moving, bustling world, two people sending their connecting glances across a crowded drawing room. They have moved, in a few heightened moments, from separate and secret yearnings to proud public acknowledgment of their future together.

Persuasion required further work, which Jane Austen surely knew. But she was unwilling or unable to commit herself to it any longer. Something at its center worried her: the character of Anne Elliot. This unfixable problem made her reluctant to apply her usual fine finishing strokes and to fill out the portraits of the lesser characters. Anne Elliot is "almost too good for me," she wrote to her niece Fanny. "Pictures of perfection" exasperated her, she claimed, and Anne with her patient fortitude and cool clarity of mind presents just such an image.

It is possible that Jane Austen's health had already begun to fail at the time of writing *Persuasion*. Just as she was finding her greatest strength as a writer, she may have experienced intimations of an early death. The darkness of *Persuasion*, its vivid sensuality, its use of accident and near misses, relates, perhaps, to the kind of fatalism that stared down at her, suggesting that she might be desperately rewriting the trajectory of her own life and giving it the gift of a happy ending. Elizabeth Bennet shared part of Austen's own rebelliousness; Emma Woodhouse embodied some of her sense of mischief; Fanny of *Mansfield Park* might be thought of as Jane Austen attempting the role of dutiful goodness, performing an act of expiation for the levity and brightness she had brought to *Pride and Prejudice*. But Anne Elliot, more than any of these heroines, combines Austen's sense of loss and loneliness, her regrets, her intelligence, and in the end, her willingness to lead a disappointed life.

A number of other tasks occupied her at the time. She had bought back the manuscript for *Northanger Abbey* for the original £10 she had been paid and was busy making a series of emendations, readying it for the press. The pressures on her were enormous. Family occupied a good deal of her time: her nieces and nephews, her brother Henry's bankruptcy and his decision to enter the Church. There were endless visitors at Chawton Cottage, family and friends who had to be accommodated. On top of this, she was not feeling well.

She was fatigued. Her back hurt, and her knee. Her nights were feverish. She took to lying down after dinner. She grew increasingly irritable, especially with the presence of young children. To family and friends she offered various forms of self-diagnosis. Her condition was caused by "bile." Or else rheumatism. Always she felt herself to be improving, and she shared each small increment of renewed strength with family members. Illness had always been a bore to her, something to push aside, and she had an abhorrence of hypochondria, a condition frequently mocked in her novels. During the winter of 1817 she gathered what energy she had and wrote twelve chapters of a new novel, a fragment not published until 1925.

Sanditon, though unfinished, shows the direction in which Jane Austen might have moved had she lived longer. In it she exploits her greatest gifts, her management of dialogue and her skill with monologue. The book feels open and modern, admitting a new and changing social landscape. Old values were giving way to a new, restless bustle of prosperity, and there is a sense that Jane Austen welcomed this new social vitality and that she may have been on the cusp of widening her novelistic scope. As vigorous and inventive as her earlier work, the fragment does not read like the work of a dying woman. The overall theme of reality and artifice is not new to Austen, but the setting is. She is writing here about the resort development of a seaside town, the invasion of the new into an old and authentic community. The comedy is broad and blunt, but the characterization, especially that of Sir Edward Denham, is more subtle and psychologically shaded than anything she had attempted.

In March, however, she was forced to give up writing, and at the end of April, an invalid by now, she quietly wrote her will. Cassandra was appointed her executrix, and it was to Cassandra that all her worldly goods would go—except for a £50 legacy to Henry and another £50 to a Madam Bigeon, a housekeeper who had looked after her sister-in-law Eliza. She had exerted herself to do those things that invalids did at the time; she visited Cheltenham to take the waters and she even attempted donkey riding as a form of exercise.

It was decided that she, and Cassandra as her nurse, should take lodgings in Winchester so she would be nearer her surgeon, Mr. Lyford. It was a rainy May day when brother James sent his carriage to take her and Cassandra on the sixteen-mile journey. Henry, always the loyal brother, accompanied them on horseback.

As ever she took an interest in her surroundings, describing with appreciation the neat little College Street drawing room with its bow window and view overlooking a garden. Weak as she was, she managed to write to her nephew James Edward Austen-Leigh a few days later, making light of her condition. Her irony is in perfect form, and so is her wish to maintain a semblance of improving health. "I will not boast of my handwriting; neither that, nor my face have yet recovered their proper beauty; but in other respects I am gaining strength very fast." This letter was dated May twenty-seventh.

By mid-June the family realized that Aunt Jane was not going to recover. She took Holy Communion along with her two clerical brothers, James and Henry, and was strong enough, it was reported, to attend to the service. Suffering from what was most likely cancer, she rallied for a few days and even dictated a number of comic verses, which have been preserved.

It is impossible to say for certain what the nature of her illness was. Claire Tomalin, the biographer, suggests a lymphoma. For quite some time Austen was believed to have suffered from Addison's disease, a tuberculosis of the adrenal glands, a condition not identified until 1860, more than forty years after Austen's death. The Addison symptoms, however, don't match well with those bodily failings Jane Austen knew. She had suffered for some months with fever and weakness and was said by one of her nieces to have grown very pale. Addison's, on the other hand, is characterized by a browning of the skin, which presents rather like the sun tan of a healthy person. It is, as well, a disease that brings on a steady decline, whereas Jane Austen's health fluctuated from day to day in the spring of 1817, and she and her family were frequently persuaded that she was recovering, then declining, then improving once again.

Breast cancer seems a very likely cause, especially since

Jane Austen's Aunt Philadelphia, and Philadelphia's daughter, Eliza, probably died from that disease. Breast cancer does appear in exactly such family clusters. The fevers Jane Austen suffered would have been consistent with the visitations of hot flushes in which the body is continually adjusting to an imbalance of estrogen.

On the seventeenth of July she suffered a seizure and died early the next morning. Cassandra closed her sister's eyes, honored, she said, to be able to perform this small service. She also cut a few locks of her hair to keep and to give to such friends as Anne Sharp.

The funeral took place early in the morning of July twenty-fourth. It was a small affair; women did not generally attend funerals at this time, since it was felt that their grief might be uncontrollable. The mourning party consisted of three of the Austen brothers and a few other male members of the family.

Jane Austen, who loved the out-of-doors, was laid to rest inside the stones of Winchester Cathedral. The inscription on her tomb reads: "The benevolence of her heart, the sweetness of her temper, and the extraordinary endowments of her mind obtained the regard of all who knew her, and the warmest love of her intimate connections." There was no mention of her six great novels, her literary offspring, her own "darling" children.

23

IMMEDIATELY AFTER Jane Austen's death she was entombed in veneration. Henry espoused her piety, her nieces recorded her skill with a needle, and Cassandra censored her correspondence so that the world would understand the angel of goodness her sister had been, that very "picture of perfection" that enraged Jane herself.

What is known of Jane Austen's life will never be enough to account for the greatness of her novels, but the point of literary biography is to throw light on a writer's works, rather than combing the works to re-create the author. The two "accounts"—the life and the work—will always lack congruency and will sometimes appear to be in complete contradiction.

Jane Austen, the stern moralist, was capable of petty cruelty; her control of her material stood at odds with her own lack of self-control. "If I am a wild Beast I cannot help it," she wrote to Cassandra. "It is not my own fault." Neat, clever Jane Austen in her lace cap a wild woman? If she is refusing blame for her own disordered self, then where might we place it? Her biological temperament may have contributed to what she perceived as wildness, or else the difficult circumstances of her life. She was poor. She was isolated. Several times she was banished from the home she loved. Her heroines claimed their lives through ideal marriages, while she found her own sense of arrival through her novels. She knew her worth as a writer, but lived, it seems, in a society that was late in recognizing what was plainly evident. And she was a physical being who had few opportunities to express that part of herself.

Did she ever know a sexual relationship beyond a stolen kiss or two at a ball? Probably not. She was conventional about marriage and fidelity, so that even a random opportunity would have tested her moral sense, causing her to hesitate. And she was extraordinarily well chaperoned all her life, so that the privacy required for a sexual liaison would be unlikely to offer itself. There seems a contemporary reluctance to believe that anyone who writes so completely about the intricacies of love should have been inexperienced about love's physical expressiveness, but Jane Austen was knowing about sexual matters, as even her juvenilia informs us, and she was for a time an enthusiastic husband hunter, if we can believe Mary Russell Mitford's rather cruel remark. Her rejection of Harris Bigg-Wither may gesture toward either a general bodily fastidiousness or a revulsion for one particular man. It is not so difficult, then, given the rather rigid behavior of her class, to believe that she remained sexually innocent, especially when it is remembered that she lived with an admired older sister who had set the pattern early in her life, and whose spinster presence could only have normalized the situation.

Austen's narrative intricacies and turns were propelled for the most part by incident or by reason, and not by the needs or responses of the body. The brain—for Jane Austen does frequently refer to that particular fleshly organ—presides over the rest of the corporeal body that is treated with what? Indifference? Incuriosity? Disregard? Or perhaps a metaphorical shrug that all but erases itself. Or else her strategy, conscious or unconscious, points to the values that she believed supported a decent community of individuals.

At the same time we are never given to believe that Jane Austen found the body repellent. The juvenilia took a rather mischievous delight in seductions and rapes, and then there was Cousin Eliza, who undoubtedly contributed a sense of the earthy to the young Jane. Later, Austen's letters reveal a pervasive and sensuous delight in fabrics, muslins, ribbons, lace. As a young woman she loved to dance, and must have felt that the movement of dance brought her alive physically, just as George Knightley is finally given his body when he dances at the local ball—for until that moment we have had nothing but his hard, reasonable head.

Everything we know of Emma and Elizabeth and Catherine—their spiritedness, their admiration for good sense and directness—tells us that they are not, by nature, a trio of prudes. Yet, except for the brain, the human body is infrequently mentioned in Jane Austen's work. The reluctance to speak of the body's parts, the body's yearnings and satisfactions, reflects particular attitudes of Austen's era, but it is also consistent with the kind of writer she was.

There is, for instance, no mention of toes in any of her work, though there are a few fingers. Nor are there any hips, thighs, shins, buttocks, kidneys, intestines, wombs, or navels, and scarcely a single mention of toothache, said to have been the most commonly feared malady among all classes of people in the eighteenth century. There are, in Jane Austen's collective work, few chins or ankles, and just an occasional nose, ear, leg, wrist, eyebrow, and eyelash. The word breast is mentioned several times, but most of these singular breasts belong to men and represent not flesh and nipple, but the center of feeling. People are rarely described in terms of their bodily posture; instead it is their *air* that is noted, a favorite Austen word, uniting substance and impression in one verbal bundle.

True, there are hundreds of eyes, hearts, and hands, but Jane Austen's eyes, hearts, and hands belong more to the eighteenth-century rational system than they do to human anatomy. Hearts record sensation, eyes are read for meaning, and hands are used metaphorically, much as we use that word, to symbolize a human transaction of one kind or another. Faces—of which there are well over a hundred mentioned—exist mainly to express reaction or convey meaning, and, in fact, the more abstract "countenance" receives even more mention and more nearly expresses Austen's meaning. In the same way, "skin" often yields to the more metaphori-

A Few Words About Sources

ALMOST AS SOON as I began to read Jane Austen's novels, I became curious about her life. Who was the woman who created Elizabeth Bennet, Fanny Price, and, my favorite, Emma Woodhouse? Where did her profound insights into human nature come from and how did she learn to animate her characters so that they leaped from the page? Someone pointed me in the direction of her nephew's 1870 memoir, the words of James Edward Austen-Leigh, which, for all its strange, obstinate gaps, is still the place to begin. (He was a favorite nephew–handsome, gifted–and his piece is illuminated with an affection that his aunt returned.) Lord David Cecil's *A Portrait of Jane Austen* (1978) is also affectionate, as though he too were a favored nephew. I could not have done without David Gilson's comprehensive *A Bibliography of Jane Austen* (1982). Marilyn Butler's *Jane Austen and the War of Ideas* (1975) is a model of scholarship, as is Mary Lascelles' *Jane Austen and Her Art* (1939), and both are wonderfully readable. Tony Tanner's *Jane Austen* (1986) is richly informative on the novels themselves. Books by Nigel Nicolson (*The World of Jane Austen,* 1991), Jean Freeman (*Jane Austen in*

Bath, 1969) and Irene Collins (*Jane Austen and the Clergy,* 1994) provided me with a much-needed sense of context.

There have been many biographies of Jane Austen, and I am grateful I have had these to lean upon. Works by Park Honan (1987) and John Halperin (1984) each brought new perspectives, as did Helen Lefroy's 1997 *Jane Austen.* In a crisp twenty-nine pages Sylvia Townsend Warner captured a brilliant life with her own sparkling prose (*Jane Austen,* 1951) and demonstrated the powers of the short, short, short biography. Every writer, established or aspiring, should read this marvelous little book. Two recent biographies have once again raised the level of Jane Austen scholarship, at the same time making the reading of literary biography a distinct pleasure. Claire Tomalin (*Jane Austen, A Life,* 1997) writes with grace and generosity, bringing new psychological insights and observations. We might wonder at times if there is anything more to be known about Jane Austen, but Tomalin has found nuances of sensibility and interpreted them wisely. David Nokes (*Jane Austen,* 1997) is both sensitive to detail and dramatic in presentation, drawing with enviable erudition on the backdrop of social history.

Jane Austen's Letters, collected and edited by Deirdre Le Faye (first published in 1995 and later updated), provides an extraordinary window onto the woman Jane Austen was. Jane Austen's letter hoard was purged by her sister Cassandra (and perhaps by others), who was either extraordinarily sensitive about the family reputation or dedicated to guarding the image of Jane-the-Saint.

I am grateful to James Atlas, the editor of Penguin Lives, and to my many friends who have entered into long and patient discussion with me about Jane Austen and offered me their theories, their interpretations, and their encouragement. My debt to Jane Austen herself is incalculable.